Skills for FAMILIES, Skills for LIFE

SECOND EDITION

Also from the Boys Town Press

Teaching Social Skills to Youth, 2nd Ed.
Teaching Social Skills to Youth with Mental Health Disorders
Working with Aggressive Youth
Common Sense Parenting®, 3rd Ed.
Common Sense Parenting of Toddlers and Preschoolers
Common Sense Parenting Learn-at-Home DVD Kit
Common Sense Parenting DVDs:
    Building Relationships
    Teaching Children Self-Control
    Correcting Misbehavior
    Preventing Problem Behavior
    Teaching Kids to Make Good Decisions
    Helping Kids Succeed in School
Parenting to Build Character in Your Teen
Adolescence and Other Temporary Mental Disorders (DVD)
Changing Children's Behavior by Changing the People,
    Places and Activities in Their Lives
Good Night, Sweet Dreams, I Love You: Now Get into Bed and Go to Sleep
The Well-Managed Classroom
Safe and Healthy Secondary Schools
Tools for Teaching Social Skills in School
More Tools for Teaching Social Skills in School
Competing with Character®
There Are No Simple Rules for Dating My Daughter
Who's Raising Your Child?
No Room for Bullies
Dealing with Your Kids' 7 Biggest Troubles
Unmasking Sexual Con Games
Practical Tools for Foster Parents
Getting Along with Others

For Adolescents

Guys, Let's Keep It Real
Little Sisters, Listen Up
Boundaries: A Guide for Teens
A Good Friend
Who's in the Mirror?
What's Right for Me?

For Pre-K to Second Grade

I Like Holidays!
Visiting My Grandmother
I Like Birthdays!
My Trip to the Zoo

For a Boys Town Press catalog, visit www.BoysTownPress.org or call 1-800-282-6657.

Boys Town National Hotline
1-800-448-3000
A crisis, resource and referral number especially for kids and parents.

Skills for FAMILIES, Skills for LIFE

SECOND EDITION

How to Help Parents and Caregivers Meet the Challenges of Everyday Living

AMY SIMPSON, M.A., PAULA KOHRT, M.ED., LINDA M. SHADOIN, M.S.W.,
JONI COOK-GRIFFIN, AND JANE L. PETERSON, M.H.D.

BOYS TOWN Press
SM

Boys Town, Nebraska

Skills for Families, Skills for Life, 2nd Edition

Published by the Boys Town Press
14100 Crawford St.
Boys Town, NE 68010

Copyright © 1999, 2010 Father Flanagan's Boys' Home

ISBN: 978-1-934490-13-6

Boys Town Press is the publishing division of Boys Town, a national organization serving children and families.

Publisher's Cataloging in Publication

Skills for families, skills for life : how to help parents and caregivers meet the challenges of everyday living / Amy Simpson … [et. al.]. -- 2nd ed. -- Boys Town, NE : Boys Town Press, c2010.

p. ; cm. + 1 CD-ROM (4 ¾ in.)

ISBN: 978-1-934490-13-6
    Previous ed., c1999, by Linda M. Shadoin, Joni Cook-Griffin and Jane L. Peterson.
    CD-ROM contains printable skill sheet checklists.
    Includes bibliographical references and index.
    Summary: Communication ; Relationships ; Education ; Housing ; Medical and mental health needs ; Money management ; Child supervision ; Formal and informal support ; Nutrition ; Abuse ; Stress ; Home safety ; Community safety ; Finding resources for families.

1. Family services--United States. 2. Family social work--United States. 3. Problem families--Services for--United States. I. Simpson, Amy. II. Shadoin, Linda M. Skills for families, skills for Life. III. Father Flanagan's Boys' Home.

HV699 .S475 2010
362.82/86—dc22   100

10 9 8 7 6 5 4 3 2 1

Table of Contents

Introduction

CHAPTER 1

A Practitioner's Guide to Teaching Living Skills to Families

John and Mary Smith are in trouble. John's monthly disability check is about to be cut, Mary is struggling to hold two jobs, and their oldest son needs to start taking an expensive medication. The family can't afford medical insurance. The couple's other two kids are struggling in school; teachers are sending notes home saying that the Smith children are disruptive and fighting with other students. The Smiths' landlord wants to raise the rent on their apartment, which is in a high-crime neighborhood, run down, and infested with cockroaches. John and Mary have no relatives in town and few friends whom they can turn to for help. In addition, the couple is having trouble managing money, working out solutions with the kids' schoolteachers, and figuring out how to seek assistance in the community. These family *caregiving challenges are making it hard for the Smiths to care for their kids. Every day, it is more difficult to hold things together.*

We live in a pressure-packed world. As parents and caregivers, we must be able to tackle many different responsibilities in order to maintain a safe, healthy household for our children. Balancing a budget, preparing nutritional meals, providing housing, and making sure children receive a proper education and necessary medical care are but a few of the many day-to-day challenges every family faces. Many families are strong enough to survive tough times. Couples and single parents who have learned basic living skills know how to get things done and keep the household running somewhat smoothly. A strong spirit of teamwork and cooperation among family members also plays a big part in a family's ability to function, and oftentimes flourish, under pressure.

When parents and caregivers aren't skilled in these areas, or haven't had the opportunities to learn the skills that are necessary to perform these functions, it can be just as damaging to the stability of the home, and the well-being of the children, as more complex issues like child behavior problems, physical or sexual abuse, and alcoholism or drug addiction. Parents and caregivers who aren't meeting their children's everyday needs might even be labeled as "neglectful," even though they are trying to do the best they can with the skills they have.

In these situations, children often suffer the most. They are dependent on their parents, or other caregivers, for not only the love, affection, understanding, and sense of self-worth that are absolutely essential for healthy development, but also the everyday necessities of life. When any of these are missing, the child suffers, both physically and emotionally. Intervention then must focus on enhancing the strengths and abilities caregivers already have, and providing them with opportunities to learn new skills or strategies that will enable them to create a safe environment for their kids.

Families have the best intentions and try to do what is right. Parents like John and Mary love their children and want what's best for them. They want their children to succeed in school. They want to provide a safe, loving home. They want to have a happy family, but they just don't know how to accomplish the tasks that will enable them to reach these goals.

For practitioners, working with these families can be a tremendous challenge. Some families may not trust professionals because of past experiences. Oftentimes, families have been criticized or have felt demeaned by helping professionals who have been forthright in telling the parents and caregivers what they are supposed to do to fix their problems. Repeated criticism and advice-giving sometimes leaves family members feeling resentful and wary. These feelings interfere with their motivation, making the practitioner's job even more difficult.

In addition, practitioners may not have learned specific techniques for teaching caregiving skills outside the realm of child discipline. For example, how many practitioners learned what to teach parents who can't or don't know how to provide their children with three nutritious meals a day? The bottom line is that there are very few resources that offer practitioners information on what daily life skills to teach when a family faces caregiving problems like arranging for transportation, meal preparation, and advocating for a child's education.

This book was written by Boys Town's In-Home Family Services staff in response to these challenges. The original edition offered treatment strategies for teaching 104 living skills in eleven caregiving areas. These areas were originally chosen because practitioners from across the country identified them as ones where families most often encounter difficulties. This second edition has expanded the caregiving areas by two to include Relationships and Community Safety, and now features a total of 132 skills. In addition, the section previously titled Social Support now includes both informal and formal supports, the Preventing Abuse chapter (formerly Sexual Abuse) addresses all forms of abuse including domestic violence, and the Medical Needs section offers skills for meeting families' mental as well as physical health needs. Practitioners will also find new family skills on applying for a job, solving landlord disputes, being a wise consumer, locating registered sex offenders, protecting against Internet and cell phone safety threats, creating a family safety plan, dealing with a landlord foreclosure, and others. Finally, a new chapter on Finding Resources for Families gives many suggestions on locating public and private, national as well as local, assistance for families in the caregiving areas.

While this book does cover Child Supervision, it does not include skills for managing child behavior and disciplining children. Boys Town's approach to parenting skills can be found in the books, *Common Sense Parenting* by Ray Burke, Ph.D., Ron Herron, and Bridget A. Barnes, and *Common Sense Parenting of Toddlers and Preschoolers* by Bridget A. Barnes and Steven M. York, M.H.D. Both books are also available as audio books on CD. Parenting techniques are demonstrated on video in the *Common Sense Parenting Learn-at-Home DVD Kit* and the *Common Sense Parenting DVD Series*. All of these resources are available from the Boys Town Press (**BoysTownPress.org** or 1-800-282-6657).

The skills in this book can be taught to parents and other caregivers in a variety of settings, and instruction can be adapted to many different family-oriented programs. Since intervention might occur in situations where children's safety and well-being are at risk, this information can be used in conjunction with treatment programs that have varying theoretical approaches in order to improve conditions in the family. The ultimate goal is to teach parents and caregivers how to make the home and family safe and how to adequately meet children's needs.

New to the second edition of this book is a CD-ROM that allows practitioners to print off copies of each of the skills and use these sheets to customize and track their skill-teaching work with individual families. Each skill page includes extra blank lines for practitioners to use if they wish to make notes, add additional steps to the skill or list local resources, phone numbers, or websites useful to their families.

Helping children and families in need is what Boys Town does. Founded in 1917 by Father Edward J. Flanagan, the home at first took in wayward or orphaned boys, providing food, shelter, schooling, and a solid foundation on which they could re-start their lives. In the late 1960s and early 1970s, as the problems of youth became more serious and complex, Boys Town developed what is now known as the Boys Town Teaching Model. Rooted in social learning theory, the Model has three components – building relationships, teaching social skills, and empowerment through self-direction. The Model is at the heart of all Boys Town programs, which offer direct care and training in the areas of education, treatment foster care, residential care, mental health care, parenting, and family preservation. While Boys Town has expanded to help boys and girls, parents, families, and child-care professionals through a wide system of services, its mission has remained essentially the same – saving children and healing families.

Boys Town's In-Home Family Services has been a leader in developing effective intervention for families in need since the program was developed in the late 1980s. In addition to providing direct care for troubled families through sites and locations around the country, the program offered training for consultants, therapists, school counselors, and other practitioners who work with families.

It was through this training that practitioners from across the country expressed their need for a guide to teaching basic (cooking, doing laundry, making appointments) and complex (managing finances, seeking assistance from community resources, providing proper medical care) life skills that parents, caregivers, and even older teens can learn. Not only did their desire for a set of skills that could help address problems in those areas prompt Boys Town to develop this living skills handbook, but many of their ideas were included in the book. For the insight and experience of these dedicated professionals, Boys Town is deeply grateful.

We hope you find this book to be a useful resource as you take on the challenge of helping troubled families. Children deserve to be healthy and safe, and by teaching useful skills to parents and other caregivers, we all move closer to achieving that goal. Boys Town knows these treatment strategies work, and by sharing them with you and others, our hope is that more and more families can find the help they need.

CHAPTER 2

The Importance of Skill Teaching

Most people assume that adults already know how to be good parents and caregivers. But anyone who has been a parent to a child can tell you that no matter how smart, dedicated, loving, and motivated a person is, parenting skills do not come naturally. Knowing how to nurture children, manage household tasks, solve life problems, and negotiate for the needs of the family are learned skills, not ones people are born with.

Where do adults learn the skills to be good parents, caregivers, and providers? Many learn these skills from their own parents; they copy what their mothers and fathers did. Parents and caregivers also learn from experience and practice, or by having someone teach them the skills they need.

However, not everyone has the opportunities to learn daily life skills while growing up or in adulthood. Having poor or few role models or resources, or being isolated from sources of information can limit learning opportunities for some adults. In these situations, parents and caregivers either develop ineffective skills or simply don't acquire the necessary skills for carrying out daily living tasks and proper caregiving.

Boys Town works with thousands of families a year, and our practitioners see firsthand the difficulties parents, caregivers, and older teens with skill deficits have in solving problems and dealing with day-to-day social and living situations. And research indicates that people who have not had the opportunity to learn social skills have a harder time interacting with others and solving problems. This type of situation can jeopardize the safety, well-being, and development of the entire family.

Fortunately, our experiences also have taught us that it is never too late for adults to learn the skills they need. Wherever there is a skill deficit, a lack of knowledge, or inappropriate use of skills for solving life problems, an opportunity exists for parents and caregivers to make changes to improve how they get along in the world. Learning just a few basic skills often can provide a foundation for solving many seemingly complex problems. (For example, learning time-management skills can help a parent do a better job of getting the kids ready for school, paying the rent when it's due, and being to work on time.)

We believe that parents and other caregivers can and must learn skills to help them meet the challenges of everyday life. To accomplish this goal, we must understand how they learn these skills and how we can best teach them.

Before teaching begins, it is important to dispel a few misconceptions that might interfere with our efforts. First, we should not assume that everyone has learned how to accomplish the many basic tasks many of us do daily, such as balancing a checkbook, making appointments, doing the laundry, or hiring a babysitter. For many adults, these seemingly routine tasks can be overwhelming and frustrating. We also should not assume that parents and caregivers know how to look for solutions to problems, or are able to break down tasks into manageable pieces. Again, not everyone has had the same experiences or opportunities earlier in life that would enable them to learn these skills. Finally, we often jump to the conclusion that because a person is of adult age, he or she is competent in using adult skills. Skill competence, however, comes from practice, experience, and observation, not age. To effectively reach out to those who still need to learn these skills, we must be aware of these assumptions and the dangers of maintaining them.

Most everything we do in life can be broken down into a set of related behaviors called a skill. Skills are sets of behaviors that, when used in a given social context, bring about a desired result. For example, the specific behaviors of nodding your head, looking at a person, and summarizing what the person has said make up the skill of listening. When this set of behaviors is used in the context of communicating with another person, it results in the act of listening.

Skills can range from simple to complex. Simple skills may consist of a few behaviors that are easy to use or carry out; complex skills may involve more numerous and difficult behaviors. For example, brushing your teeth, cleaning a toilet, or introducing yourself are somewhat simple skills. Accessing public assistance, handling a landlord dispute, or advocating for a child's education are more complex skills.

Regardless of whether the skill you are teaching is simple or complex, you must recognize that most adults, like children, learn systematically and individually. The best teaching process, then, gives the learner time to absorb and understand one point before going on to another. Teaching that is focused, proceeds from specific to general information, follows a step-by-step order, and "shapes" behavior through repetition and practice will provide the biggest benefit for learners. Our practitioners find that skill-based teaching that introduces one behavior at a time enables parents, caregivers, and teens to learn and retain both simple and complex skills. Boys Town has developed many techniques for teaching skills, and the more opportunities for learning that can be created, the better the chances are that adults will pick them up. (These teaching techniques are explained in detail in the Boys Town book, *Building Skills in High-Risk Families: Strategies for the Home-Based Practitioner,* by Jane L. Peterson, M.H.D., Paula Kohrt, M.Ed., Linda M. Shadoin, M.S.W., and Karen Authier, M.S.W.)

In any teaching you do with a family, it is imperative that family members are not blamed for what they can't do. It is difficult for parents and caregivers to admit that they don't know how to properly prepare meals or monitor their children or obtain medical care when necessary. If your approach offends your clients or makes them feel like they can't do anything right, chances are you won't get very far. Here are some important guidelines that are essential for successful skill teaching:

Start where the person is. Assess the person's individual learning style, strengths, and limitations. Everyone has different experiences and cognitive abilities, and everyone learns at a different pace. Take this into consideration when choosing which skills to teach.

Begin with what is important to the person. No one wants to learn skills that aren't related to what he or she wants or hopes to accomplish. Identify the person's goals and partner them with skills that will help him or her achieve the desired changes. Resist the temptation to teach skills you think are important, but which aren't necessarily critical for the parents and caregivers, or the well-being of the children.

Build on family members' strengths. Use what they know or what they do well as a base for learning new skills. Find out what a family member is good at and teach skills that are related to these strengths. Learning happens faster and a person is more likely to remember a skill if it is tied into experiences and strengths he or she already has.

Connect what family members are learning to their goals. Explaining why it is important to learn new skills in terms of what the family will gain helps members to be more invested and motivated. If family members don't see the benefit in trying something new, they will be less likely to take the steps toward change.

Through your teaching, family members can find success in learning new skills and improving the ones they already know. With careful attention on the learning process, and the strengths and goals of the family, the skills you teach can go far in helping parents, caregivers, and teens solve problems, meet needs, and improve relationships.

CHAPTER 3

How the Skills in This Book Are Organized

Practitioners take on an awesome responsibility every time they walk into a family's life. Oftentimes, the knowledge and dedication they bring into a home helps set a new course for how family members will function and care for each other in the future.

So far, we've focused on why it's important for families to learn living skills. Now it's time to look at the specific problem areas where many families need help and the skills that can be taught in each area. This chapter explains how this material will be presented.

Each of the next thirteen chapters will focus on one of the following problem areas: communication, relationships, education, housing, medical and mental health needs, money management, child supervision, informal and formal support, nutrition, abuse, stress, home safety, and community safety. Each chapter offers an introduction that explains the problem area, followed by a list of skills that can be taught in that area. Under each skill heading is a list of component behaviors or steps that comprise the skill.

Many of the same skills can be used to address different problem areas. For quick reference, a table that shows which living skills can be taught in each area is provided at the end of this book. Some of the skills are similar to those found in the book, *Teaching Social Skills to Youth*, by Tom Dowd and Jeff Tierney, which offers 182 skills and their steps. (These adapted skills are marked with the symbol *.)

The skills are presented in a generic manner so practitioners can choose which of the component behaviors a parent, caregiver, or teen must learn in order to successfully use the skill. Some behaviors may be too complex for the family members you are working with, so they may need to be broken down into simpler components to make them easier to understand and learn. For example, the behavior "Arrange transportation, if necessary" is listed under the skill of keeping medical or mental health appointments. If a person doesn't know how to arrange for transportation, this step may have to be taught as a separate skill before you can teach how to keep appointments.

When teaching these skills, it is important to be flexible, both in the way you teach and in what you teach. Adapt your teaching to best meet the needs of the learner. The behavior lists for each skill are extensive, but not inclusive. For example, in order to effectively help the family or person with whom you are working, it may be necessary to add behavior steps, or teach the steps in a different order. In addition, the wording of a skill or a behavior should be changed to fit the language the person uses. If the behavior of a skill says "State your opinion in a calm voice," you may change the wording of this step to something like "Stay cool, and tell the person what is bugging you," if that is closer to the language the family member uses.

We have tried to make each skill and the related behaviors easy to understand. Behavior steps are based on current and common knowledge about the best treatment approaches for the problem areas. If you don't know why certain behaviors are being suggested, take time to learn more about the problem area and the typical treatment approaches. For example, if you aren't sure why it is important for sexual abuse victims to set clear boundaries in relationships, learn more about sexual abuse. The more knowledge you have about specific problem areas and the benefits of acquiring new skills, the more effective your teaching will be. Time spent researching each topic area should enhance the learning process and help family members pick up skills more quickly. Chapter 17, Finding Resources for Families, lists many organizations and websites offering extensive information that can be useful to you.

The skills included in this book can be used as a guide for teaching families useful approaches to dealing with a number of caregiving challenges. But practitioners should be aware that there are limitations to their effectiveness in any particular situation. Boys Town cannot guarantee that teaching the skills presented will result in the desired outcomes for the families with whom you work. Common sense should be exercised when choosing, adapting, and teaching these skills. Also, these skills are not intended to replace or overrule the advice and sound judgment of qualified professionals such as doctors, counselors, pharmacists, or teachers. It is highly recommended that practitioners incorporate the teaching of skills within a well-rounded intervention that allows for individualized assessment and treatment planning.

It is important for practitioners to accept that family members are doing the best they can with the skills they have. If parents and caregivers need to do better, then we are responsible for teaching the right skills the right way so that they can make changes that will benefit them and their family. By providing the many skill options in this book, it is our hope that you and parents, caregivers, or teens can choose skills that will help families successfully meet the challenges of everyday living.

Problem
Areas

CHAPTER 4

Communication

PROBLEM: Family members have difficulty communicating with others.

Most families encounter problems communicating and relating to one another on occasion. Knowing how to share feelings, express opinions, and disagree without arguing are skills that everyone needs to know and practice in order to get along with others. Many of us have experienced or witnessed the negative results of poor communication between two people: arguments, name-calling, accusations, and, sometimes, physical fights. When family members are unable to appropriately state their feelings, wants, or needs, frustration increases and problems are left unresolved. A person with poor communication skills also often has difficulty relating to others on the job, in the home, and in the community. Over time, unresolved conflicts can lead to severe consequences like running away, divorce, and getting fired.

In order to prevent conflicts, solve problems, and work through disagreements, family members must be able to effectively communicate with one another and others. Also, communication skills are key to getting one's needs met. People who can listen and understand what others are saying, as well as express themselves clearly, benefit from the give and take of effective communication. There are several communication skills a person can learn to improve relationships, solve problems, and get personal needs met.

Identifying Own Feelings *

- Take a moment to think about what you are feeling.

- Consider the situation that is connected with your feeling.

- Determine how your body feels when you encounter the situation (e.g., upset stomach, light-headed, tensed muscles, relaxed).

- Label the feeling with one word that best describes it (e.g., anger, sadness, confusion, joy, excitement, happiness, surprise).

- List how your feelings change with different situations and experiences.

- Identify and label various feelings as they arise.

- Describe your feelings so others can understand them.

Active Listening

- Look at the person who is talking.

- Occasionally summarize what you understand the person has said.

- Ask if what you have summarized is accurate.

- Ask the person to explain if he or she uses a word or makes a statement that is unclear.

- Wait until the person is done talking to respond or ask a question.

Expressing Feelings

- Explain to the person that you would like to talk about how you are feeling.

- Identify the feelings you want to talk about.

- Determine when you feel this way (e.g., think about the events that occur before you experience these feelings).

- Remain calm.

- State your feelings by saying, "I feel ... when happens." Avoid starting statements with, "You make me feel...."

- Take a deep breath to help you relax if the feelings become more intense.

- Thank the person for listening.

- Allow the other person to respond to your statement.

Asking Others for Opinions

- Explain the problem or situation to the other person.

- Ask if the person has any ideas or suggestions about your situation.

- Ask for clarification if you don't understand the person's opinion. Do not argue or criticize any suggestions.

- Thank the person for sharing his or her opinion.

- Decide later whether or not to make changes based on the person's opinions.

Apologizing *

- Determine what you did wrong and who was affected by your behavior.

- Using a sincere voice, tell the other person you would like to apologize.

- Begin by saying, "I want to apologize for..." or "I'm sorry for...."

- Take responsibility for everything you did wrong. Do not make excuses or give reasons for why you did what you did.

- Clearly state what you did.

- Explain that you will try to avoid making the same mistake again.

- If you took or damaged something, offer to replace or repair it.

- Follow through with your offer.

Being Assertive *

- Decide what you want to say and to whom.

- Use a calm and neutral tone of voice.

- Clearly state your opinion, request, or disagreement.

- Take time to listen to the other person's response.

- Acknowledge the other person's viewpoint.

Making a Request *

- Politely and calmly ask the person what you would like him or her to do.

- State the request in the form of a question (e.g., "Would you please...?").

- Be specific about when and how the person can do what you are asking.

- If necessary, explain the reason for the request in two sentences or less.

- If your request is granted, thank the person.

- Be prepared to accept a "No" answer.

Giving an Instruction

- Politely and calmly tell the person what you would like him or her to do.

- Be specific and clear.

- Ask to make sure the person understands your instruction.

- Check to see if the person followed the instruction to your satisfaction.

- Thank the person for following your instruction.

Stating Expectations

- Decide what your expectations are. That is, what do you want to have happen?

- Clearly tell the person what you expect.

- Be specific about how the other person can meet your expectations. For instance, clearly state what the person should do, when and how.

- Provide brief reasons (two sentences or less) for why you have set each expectation.

- Answer any questions the person may have about your expectations.

- Write down the expectations to prevent confusion or arguments.

Saying "No" *

- Decide if you want to say "No" to someone's request and why.

- In a calm, clear, and firm voice, say "No."

- If the person refuses to accept your "No" answer, leave the situation.

- If you choose to give a reason, briefly explain why you said "No" (in two sentences or less).

Correcting Another Person *

- Identify the other person's behaviors or actions you want to correct.

- Use a calm and pleasant voice tone.

- Begin with a positive statement ("I liked that you …") or an empathy statement ("I understand that it is hard to …").

- Specifically describe the behaviors the person is using that you think should be corrected.

- Briefly explain why the behavior should be corrected (in two sentences or less).

- Listen to the person's response.

- Answer any questions the person may have about what he or she is doing.

Responding to Accusations *

- Remain calm as the person is talking to you.

- Listen to everything the other person says.

- Let the person know that you understand what he or she is saying or that a problem exists.

- Wait until the person is done talking before you respond.

- Answer the accusation truthfully by either admitting or denying the accusation.

- Determine if you need to work with the person to resolve a problem or if you need to apologize.

- If necessary, make a plan for resolving the problem.

Ending an Argument

- Identify when you or the person you are talking to begins to argue. Look for signs such as yelling, screaming, name-calling, interrupting, and disagreeing with one another.

- Be aware of whether your feelings are becoming more intense and negative.

- Decide if you need to end the conversation or take a time-out.

- Tell the other person that you do not want to argue and would like to discuss the issue at another time.

- If the other person wants to discuss the issue later, agree on a time after everyone has had a chance to think and calm down.

- Stop talking and, if necessary, leave the room.

Preparing for a Discussion

- Think through what you may want to say.

- Write down the important information you want to remember to discuss.

- Make sure the issues you want to discuss are stated fairly.

- Practice assertively saying what you want to say.

- Think about how other people in the discussion might respond.

- Decide how you will respond to other people's objections or concerns.

- If you begin to get nervous, practice relaxation techniques, such as deep-breathing.

Negotiating *

- Identify what issue(s) you disagree on.

- Offer to discuss the issue to work out a solution.

- Ask the person to explain his or her viewpoint about the issue.

- Calmly explain your viewpoint to the other person.

- Discuss possible compromises each of you would be willing to make.

- Together, choose the best compromise solution(s).

- Decide when and how the compromise will be implemented.

Writing a Contract

- Decide what conditions or requirements will be included in the contract. Each person involved in the contract should have an equal number of items so that the contract is balanced.

- Write the contract in the first person, using statements like, "I, John, agree to...."

- Write the most difficult items in the contract first.

- Write each item in clear and specific terms in order to prevent confusion.

- Identify who is responsible for fulfilling each condition or requirement in the contract.

- Include short time lines for completing the conditions or requirements.

- If including consequences or rewards in the contract, determine who will deliver and receive them, and when.

- Include a specific time for when the contract will be reviewed and revised, if necessary.

- Make sure everyone who is involved in the contract agrees to the terms as they are written.

- Make any necessary revisions so that everyone agrees to the contract's conditions.

- Have everyone sign and date the contract.

- Give each person a copy of the contract or post it where everyone can see it.

Holding Family Meetings

- Schedule the meeting when all family members can attend.

- Sit in a room where everyone can be comfortable and feel included.

- Establish or review the rules for the meeting (take turns talking, don't blame others, parents have the final decision-making authority).

- Set a time limit for the meeting.

- List the issues that will be discussed.

- Limit the number of issues to be discussed.

- Take turns sharing ideas and opinions about each issue.

- Give everyone an opportunity to speak.

- If necessary, solve problems together.

- Plan activities or a new course of action to resolve any issues.

Showing Appreciation *

- Identify what the other person has done that you appreciate.

- Thank the person in a sincere voice tone.

- Specifically describe what the person has done that you appreciate.

- Provide a brief reason for why you appreciate what the person did.

- Offer future help or favors in return.

Praising

- Determine what the person did that is worthy of recognition.

- Express your approval by making a simple praise statement like, "Great job!", "Super!", or "Nice work!"

- Tell the person what he or she did well; be specific so the person will know what you liked.

- Explain why what the person did was good and how it will help him or her in the future.

Giving a Compliment *

- Speak with a clear and enthusiastic voice.

- Tell the person specifically what you like about the person, his or her behavior, or his or her project.

- Allow the person to respond to your compliment.

CHAPTER 5

Relationships

PROBLEM: Families have strained relationships between spouses, siblings, and/or parent and child.

Parents can become so overwhelmed by financial difficulties, substance use, or the many demands of daily life that relationships within the family deteriorate. Or, they may have grown up in dysfunctional families themselves without good role models for healthy relationships. As a result, many family interactions end up being mostly negative. Homes can be filled with nagging, belittling, criticizing, arguing, and even fighting. Siblings may vie for parents' attention. Struggling parents may talk to each other only about problems or crises that must be somehow managed. There may be few enjoyable family activities and kids are left on their own to fill their days.

Such families need to be taught how to improve relationships within the home, and they must learn to do more than just reduce negative behaviors. Spouses and partners must be affectionate and caring with each other and toward their children. If they can view themselves as a team, taking on the family's challenges may not seem so difficult. Having fun together as a family can be encouraged by planning simple but special activities and outings. Children can be taught to share and take turns, play nicely with their siblings, and make friends outside the family. Teaching parents the power of praise and empathy can go a long way toward building stronger family relationships and brightening the social climate inside the home.

Strengthening the Relationship with Your Spouse

- Focus on your spouse's positive qualities rather than his or her faults.

- Communicate with your spouse – share the day's successes as well as frustrations or disappointments, discuss and solve problems, and make plans and set goals together.

- Recognize the importance of teamwork in a marriage – decide on roles and responsibilities for each spouse, ask for help when you need it from your partner.

- Regularly schedule some time together where you can be "husband-and-wife" and not "parents" first.

- Treat and speak to your spouse with respect – give compliments, apologize, ask rather than demand, think twice before criticizing, etc.

- Make a plan to address the family's finances – set financial goals, develop a family budget and plans for managing debt and building a credit history, organize financial records, and monitor spending.

- Develop a written plan on what you will do when conflict arises – what you are willing to do to solve the problem.

- When you have disagreements, discuss them calmly and privately, not in front of the children.

Seeking Marriage or Family Counseling

- Identify as clearly as you can the underlying

family or relationship issue that is troubling you –
for example, financial problems could be stressing
the marriage, an affair could create a lack of trust
between partners, or family responsibilities may
not be equally shared.

- Consider what resources are available to the family
  – a marital counselor, anger control group, pastor
  or church, couples support group, marriage
  enhancement classes, other respected married
  couples, child or respite care, financial planner,
  parents' night out events, mental health facility.

- Select the service or group that appears most
  appropriate to helping you address your problem.

- Schedule an appointment with a professional or
  attend a support group, class, or event together as
  a couple.

- Periodically evaluate whether your relationship is
  improving and the counseling or support group
  you have chosen is working for you. If not, decide
  whether a different approach should be tried.

Improving Relationships with Your Children

- Play with and read to infants and toddlers to bond
  with children and encourage their growth and
  development.

- As children grow, spend time together as a family
  and have fun: Schedule one "family night" each
  week to talk, play games, or share hobbies.

- Take time for special activities you can do with
  each child individually.

- Listen when your children come to you with
  problems or questions.

- Talk *with* your children, not *at* them.

- Set reasonable expectations for your children's
  behavior. Learn what is reasonable to expect from
  each of your children by talking to their
  pediatrician or school teachers, borrowing a book
  on child development from the library, or checking

out parenting websites. Demanding that children perform tasks or behave in ways beyond their capabilities will only create unnecessary stress and anger in the home.

- Notice and praise your children for the good things they do. Try to have four of these positive interactions with a child for every one time you must correct or criticize his or her behavior.

- Show physical affection to your children with hugs, kisses, pats on the back, and "high fives."

- Set reasonable limits on your children's behavior. If they are old enough, ask them to discuss and help decide with you what the house rules and penalties for breaking them should be.

- Follow through and be fair with positive and negative consequences for their good and bad behavior.

- When you must correct a child's behavior, start with a statement of empathy such as, "I see that you're upset right now, but ..." or "I know you'd rather be outside playing with your friends, but ..."

Helping Siblings Get Along with Each Other

- Explain to your children how you expect them to play, work, and share with each other and give them opportunities to practice skills such as taking turns, solving problems, and saying "Please" and "Thank you."

- Reward your children when they do get along or help each other by praising or giving them an extra privilege or treat.

- Tell them ahead of time the negative consequences (extra chores, loss of privileges) they will earn if they argue or fight with their siblings.

- Consider using negative consequences that require them to cooperate (such as a joint chore or removing a toy or game and asking them to come up with a plan on how to share it in the future).

- Don't expect your children to be as skilled, interested, or talented as each other in the same areas, and don't compare them to their siblings.

- Enjoy your children's differences and compliment and praise them for their unique interests and skills.

Helping Children Make New Friends

- Teach children the skills they will need to "break the ice" with new acquaintances – to offer a greeting, to introduce and give some information about themselves, to ask the other child for information ("What's your name?" or "What school do you go to?"), and to invite participation ("Wanna play catch?").

- Help children behave positively toward others by teaching them skills such as expressing interest in others, giving compliments, saying "Please" and "Thank you," offering help and comfort, cooperating, sharing, and taking turns.

- Get to know the parents of your child's acquaintances and classmates and arrange play dates for your child with one or two other children at a time.

- Encourage your kids to invite their friends over and make them welcome in your home. Monitor their activities and behavior when they are with other children.

- Encourage your children's participation in social and healthy activities in the neighborhood, community, school, and church.

CHAPTER 6

Education

PROBLEM: Children's educational needs are not being adequately met.

A variety of factors may lead to a situation where a child's educational needs are not being met. In some cases, a child's parents may not know about or be able to obtain the necessary support, information, or resources for the child's education. In other cases, the school system does not offer the child educational opportunities that fit the child's special learning needs. Although parents are ultimately responsible for overseeing that educational needs are met, school systems have a legal responsibility to offer the services that best educate the child. Therefore, school issues often require a cooperative effort between the parents and the school. All parents and caregivers need skills that will help them communicate effectively with school personnel. Parents also may need information about their legal rights and support resources. This is especially true when a child has a learning disability or other special education needs. Sometimes, the situation may require parents to use child-management skills in order to motivate the child to attend and fully participate in school. Skills for assisting the parent or caregiver in dealing with school issues and problems are provided here.

Checking on a Child's School Progress

- Identify important school personnel with whom you should meet. This includes the child's teachers, the principal, counselors, the school secretary (who schedules appointments), and possibly others.

- Introduce yourself to school professionals and tell them who your child is.

- Tell the professionals that you want to work with them to ensure your child's success in school. Encourage them to contact you with any concerns that might arise.

- Determine how often you should contact school personnel. Base your decision on your child's needs and the teacher's schedule.

- Make a plan for maintaining contact with school personnel (e.g., weekly phone calls or e-mails to the guidance counselor, school notes, assignment books).

- Make a special plan to work together with the school when problems in the child's school performance or behavior arise. Contact school officials more frequently, if necessary.

Monitoring a Child's Homework

- Find out what assignments the child has to complete at home and when the assignments are due.

- Set clear expectations for completing homework (assignments must be done before watching TV; the child must study for one hour, four nights a week).

- Choose a place where the child can complete homework without being bothered.

- Check the homework when it is completed.

- Have the child complete any unanswered or incorrect parts of homework assignments.

- Frequently contact the child's teacher or school guidance counselor to confirm that the child is completing homework assignments.

Using a Daily Assignment Book

- In a notebook or assignment book, create a log of the child's assignments for each class, including due dates, dates completed, and comments. Add spaces where you and the teacher can sign off on assignments.

- Clearly explain to the child that he or she is responsible for using the assignment book to keep track of schoolwork.

- Talk with teachers about how the child will use the assignment book and what they should do with it on a daily basis.

- Check the child's daily homework assignments that are listed in the book. Check the book every day to ensure that assignments are completed correctly and on time.

- Sign off on completed assignments and write any comments for the teacher in the book.

- Make sure the child and the teacher are using the assignment book as intended.

- Establish a plan between you, the child, and the teacher to decide what will happen when assignments aren't being done and when they are successfully completed.

Monitoring a Child's School Attendance

- Contact the school and find out who keeps track of student attendance.

- Introduce yourself and tell the staff person your child's name.

- Ask about your child's attendance.

- Contact the school regularly if you need to verify your child's school attendance.

- Learn about the school's attendance policy.

- Call the school to report when your child is going to be absent.

- Notify the school if you find out that your child skipped school.

Getting Involved with a Child's School

- Attend scheduled meetings, conferences, and open houses at the school.

- When visiting the school, introduce yourself to your child's teachers, the school principal, and other people involved in your child's education.

- Ask for a copy of the school handbook and be sure your child follows the school rules.

- Volunteer to help in your child's classroom or with class activities when your schedule will allow.

- Make arrangements to visit the school and your child's classroom.

- Find out about extracurricular activities that you and your child can participate in (sports, booster clubs, Parent-Teacher Association, drama club, and fundraisers).

Communicating with School Personnel

- Prepare for the meeting or discussion with school personnel by writing down what you want to say and questions you would like answered.

- Think about how you can state your concerns in a positive manner that shows that you would like to agree on a solution.

- Schedule a time to talk with school personnel that is convenient for everyone.

- Clearly state your concerns and ask how you and school personnel can deal with the problems together.

- Stay calm and positive throughout the conversation. Avoid blaming or becoming defensive.

- Ask the school representative to clarify any school "lingo" – language used by educators that you may not understand.

- Thank the representative for working with you to meet the educational needs of your child.

- Schedule a follow-up meeting, if necessary.

Visiting a Child's School

- Call the school for information on its visitation policy.

- If you want an extended visit at the school, schedule the visit in advance.

- Arrange for a tour of the school and your child's classroom.

- Go to the school and check in at the office.

- When visiting the child's classroom, introduce yourself to the teacher. Ask how you can best observe without disrupting the class.

- When the teacher has time, ask any questions you may have about the classroom, the teaching of material, or your child's progress.

Cooperating with the School When a Child Breaks a Rule

- Find out from the teacher, principal, or counselor what your child did wrong and what action the school has already taken.

- Ask your child to describe the situation and the behavior that got him or her in trouble.

EDUCATION

- If necessary, review the school handbook to understand the rule(s) that may have been broken.

- Consider how you will show support for the school (giving your child a consequence, establishing more rules, monitoring your child's school progress or behavior more closely).

- Make an appointment with the teacher, principal, or counselor to discuss any concerns or questions you may have about the incident.

- Talk to school personnel about what they will do if your child breaks the rule again.

- Let the school personnel know that you support their decisions.

- Offer to work out a plan with the school for preventing the problem from happening again.

Choosing an Education Program

- Have your child's learning needs assessed through the use of evaluations, teacher reports, and school records.

- Find out about your child's rights and the time lines you must follow for special education services.

- Ask for recommendations from as many professionals as necessary to determine which types of education programs are best suited for your child.

- Check out education options by gathering available information about each program.

- Consider the advantages and disadvantages to each program.

- Choose the program that best fits your child's educational needs and strengths.

- Occasionally evaluate your child's progress in the programs you choose.

Advocating for a Child's Education

- Identify the child's educational needs. Ask for opinions from the child's teachers, counselor, principal, doctor, and other adults whom the child encounters on a regular basis.

- Request assistance from the school's special education staff for assessments, evaluations, and education planning.

- Request copies of the child's school records, including the results of any testing or evaluations.

- Get professional advice from objective persons (e.g., private practitioners or education specialists outside of the school system).

- Research the child's rights and find out who is responsible (school, parent, special education program, etc.) for each aspect of the child's education.

- Obtain support from organizations that assist parents of students.

- Ask school officials or staff to ensure that the child's educational needs are met.

- Continue to insist that the educational services the child needs are provided.

- Be involved in all meetings and decisions regarding the child's educational program.

- Make decisions that are based on the child's best interests.

- If necessary, hire an attorney who is qualified to handle education cases to represent your child.

Registering a Child for School

- Contact the school to find out the time and place for registration, and registration requirements.

- Take necessary steps to meet registration requirements (e.g., have the child properly immunized, gather previous school records, find

EDUCATION

43

the child's birth certificate or a copy of it, and get money to pay registration fees).

- If special assistance is needed for registration-related fees, ask school personnel about income-based discounts and waivers.

- Go to the school during the designated registration times. Consider taking the child with you if he or she has never been to the school, or if he or she needs to learn how to find classrooms.

- Fill out registration forms and pay any fees that are due.

- Get a copy of the school's policies and rules.

- Find out when the child should arrive for the first day of school and where he or she should go.

- If possible, arrange to take a tour of the school and the child's classroom.

Hiring a Tutor

- Explore options for locating qualified tutors. Use the phone book, ask school personnel for references, and check with "learning assistance" companies.

- Choose two or three potential tutors to interview.

- Develop a list of questions to ask the tutors.

- Interview each tutor individually.

- Have the tutor meet the child and observe how they interact.

- Choose the tutor that you feel is best qualified.

- Discuss details of what services the tutor will provide to the child.

- Arrange a meeting between school personnel, the tutor, and yourself to establish an education plan for the tutor to follow.

- Determine who will pay for the tutoring services and how payments will be made.

Enrolling in a General Equivalency Diploma (GED) or Career Training Program

- Call a local public high school or community college to get the location and phone number of the nearest GED program office.

- If you are interested in career training, contact local training schools and community colleges to investigate the programs offered.

- Make a list of questions you would like to know about the GED or training program. (For example: When and where are the classes held? What does the program cost? How does one register?)

- Contact the GED or training program office by telephone or by visiting in person during business hours.

- Tell the staff person that you are interested in obtaining your GED (or in helping your child obtain his or her GED), earning an associate's degree, or enrolling in a career training course.

- Ask the questions you have.

- Write down the information you receive.

- Before choosing a training course, research your career choice: Are jobs available in your area? Will a job in this field create conflicts in caring for your children (for example, working night shifts with no child care available)? What is starting pay in the field?

- Consider your research and the advice you receive, and then decide whether to register and begin classes.

EDUCATION

CHAPTER 7

Housing

PROBLEM: The family is homeless or needs to find different housing.

Having a home that provides shelter is a basic human need. When families with children are homeless or need to find different living quarters, this need becomes urgent. Practitioners also might face situations where older teens and young adults are moving out of their parents' homes, and may not know how to find affordable housing. Being without a place to call home creates much stress and can have a disruptive impact on the family's life. Finding housing often becomes a priority when a practitioner is working with a family or a teen who does not have a place to live. The process of locating and getting situated in a new home is time-consuming and requires great effort. Because of the numerous tasks involved in moving into a new residence, families will benefit from receiving assistance and support from others.

If a family has a pattern of frequently moving or being homeless, it indicates that the family may need to learn skills in

47

how to locate and maintain appropriate housing arrangements. Families may also need help in learning how to get repairs done, deal appropriately with landlords, or handle a landlord foreclosure. (Check the Money Management chapter for skills relating to overall financial health.) Here are just a few of the skills a family might need in order to settle into and maintain a home that meets its needs.

Finding Housing

- Determine how much money your family can afford to invest in rent or house payments each month.

- Explore options for assistance that can help pay for housing. Contact the local housing authority or welfare office for information.

- Identify housing needs such as location, size, access to services, and layout of the home.

- Explore available housing options by reading ads in the newspaper, reading real estate or rental publications, driving through neighborhoods looking for rental signs, calling the housing authority office for information or assistance, calling local realtors, or asking friends or relatives.

- Pick several housing possibilities.

- Prepare a list of questions about the property, such as the amount of rent, utility costs, lease length, number of bedrooms, and pet policy.

- Call each location and speak with the manager/ owner.

- Interview the manager over the phone to see if the home meets your family's needs.

- Set up an appointment to view the property if it meets your family's initial needs.

- Make a list of references from previous landlords (or other responsible persons, such as employers) and take it to the meeting.

- Tour the property and determine if it is what you want.

- Ask about the application process if you are interested in the housing.

- Follow the steps that the landlord requires, such as filling out an application and making a deposit.

- If necessary, ask the landlord if you can make the deposit over time or if you must pay it all at once.

- Before signing a lease, make sure it states in writing who is responsible for cleaning or making repairs to the home to get it ready for move-in day.

Signing a Lease

- Read the lease thoroughly.

- Make sure the lease includes your financial and legal obligations, any rules and policies, and the owner's obligations and responsibilities.

- Ask questions about statements in the lease that are unclear.

- Have the landlord include any verbal agreements in the written lease.

- Sign and date the lease.

- Observe the landlord sign and date the lease.

- Take a copy of the lease with you for your records.

Getting Utility Services Started
(water, gas, electricity, telephone, trash, sewer)

- Call the utility company.

- Give your name and new address.

- Ask about deposits and hook-up fees. Check on using deposits that were made at a prior residence.

- Tell the utility company the date you want the service started.

- If a deposit is required before service begins, arrange to get the deposit to the company as soon as possible.

HOUSING

- If financial assistance is needed to cover hook-up costs, ask about utility assistance from state agencies, charitable organizations, or the utility company.

Notifying Others of a Change of Address

- Make a list of all persons who would need to know your new address. On the list, include all creditors, relatives, friends, utility companies, and banks you currently use. Consider listing all people or businesses you have received mail from in the last two months, including your child's school.

- Pick up change-of-address forms at the post office.

- Notify the post office of your new address and the date when your mail should be forwarded to your new address.

- Fill out a change-of-address form for each person on your list and mail it to the person.

- Some companies have toll-free numbers you can call for immediate notification of an address change. When calling these numbers, have your account numbers ready.

- If you receive a bill that is forwarded from your old address, write your new address on the bill when you send it in for payment.

Fulfilling a Lease or Rental Agreement

- Make a plan for consistently paying the rent on time.

- If a rent payment is going to be late, give the landlord as much advance notice as possible. Pay as much of the rent as possible on the due date, and pay the remainder as soon as you are able.

- Observe all rules outlined in the lease.

- Keep your home reasonably neat. Avoid health or safety hazards.

- Respect your neighbors.
- Discuss any problems promptly and calmly with your landlord.

Using Temporary Housing (Homeless Shelters)

- Call and/or go directly to the shelter with personal items such as clothes, toiletries, and important papers. Do not bring furniture.
- Ask about the specific rules for living in the shelter.
- Ask about the time limit for living in the shelter.
- Keep valuables with you at all times or have the staff store them in a safe location.
- Treat others and the property of the shelter with respect.
- Use the shelter's services that help place residents into permanent housing.

Handling Landlord Disputes

- Make sure the terms of your lease are clear and that you understand both your responsibilities and those of your landlord.
- Be sure that repairs really are the responsibility of the landlord; if damage resulted from your negligence or destructive actions, the landlord is not liable.
- Keep communication with your landlord open. See if you can resolve problems by calmly talking it over first.
- Ask for needed repairs in writing, and keep a dated copy of your request and any response from your landlord.
- If repeated repair requests are ignored, you may be able to have the local building inspector declare the apartment "uninhabitable." This may help you break a lease or withhold rent until repairs are made.

HOUSING

- Be extremely careful before withholding rent. Laws vary, and in some states withholding rent can get you evicted.

- If you cannot resolve a dispute, seek mediation by calling the mayor or city manager's office and asking for the staff member who handles "landlord-tenant mediation matters" or "housing disputes."

- If mediation fails and your dispute involves money (for example, return of a security deposit), going to small claims court where you are not required to bring an attorney may be an option.

- Seek advice from your local legal aid society.

Being Prepared for a Landlord Foreclosure

- Watch for signs that your landlord is having financial difficulties: Has the property rapidly deteriorated? Have repairs stopped being made?

- Check the Better Business Bureau to see if complaints have been made against the landlord.

- Go to the county courthouse or its website to see if any foreclosure actions or judgments have been made against the landlord.

- Save money in an emergency fund to help if you are suddenly forced to find new housing.

Responding to a Landlord Foreclosure

- If you receive notice of a foreclosure on your rental, call the sheriff's department first to find out how long the process will take.

- Find out what your state's rental laws are; some may allow tenants a grace period of thirty days or more to find new housing. The U.S. Department of Housing and Urban Development (HUD) has information on state laws at **hud.gov**.

- Contact the lender or the lender's lawyer (their name will be on the eviction notice) to find out your options. Some lenders (Fannie Mae, Freddie Mac, and others) will allow you to sign a new lease with them until the property is sold or will offer cash to assist you in moving.

- If you are nervous or uncomfortable contacting the lender directly, find a local nonprofit housing counseling agency by going to the HUD website or calling 1-800-569-4287.

CHAPTER 8

Medical and Mental Health Needs

PROBLEM: Children's medical or mental health needs are not being adequately met.

Tending to the medical needs of a healthy child requires a high level of skill and support. Even more skill and support is required to take care of a child who is sick, handicapped, or suffering from a chronic disease or mental illness. Many parents and caregivers would claim that it is often difficult to know what to do for a sick child or one with serious emotional or behavioral problems. For most people, it is confusing and intimidating to work with doctors, counselors or therapists, insurance companies, and hospital systems. When a parent is unsure of how to provide appropriate care for a child's physical, mental, and/or emotional needs, the child's health and safety can be jeopardized.

Children who are physically ill, or have disabilities or severe emotional problems, are at the greatest risk of harm from more serious health problems in situations where proper medical and mental health care is absent. The healthy growth and development of infants also may be hindered when there is a lack of appropriate medical care. When parents and caregivers have the skills to recognize the medical and mental health needs of the child, and know how to provide or obtain care, the child has the best opportunity to thrive.

Here are some common skills for meeting the basic medical, dental, and mental health needs of a child.

Recognizing Medical Needs

- Observe and note when the child displays unusual physical symptoms (fever, sweating, pulling at ears, coughing) or complains of unusual symptoms (headaches, stomachaches, diarrhea).

- If the child is able to talk, ask him or her about the level of pain or discomfort, how long symptoms have been occurring, and whether other symptoms are present ("Show me where it hurts"; "When did it start hurting?").

- Check for other symptoms the child may not be aware of (skin discoloration, rashes, bruises, swelling).

- Ask yourself if the symptoms seem normal or abnormal for the child's age and the activities he or she has been involved in.

- If the child's symptoms are abnormal or unexplainable, decide if medical attention is needed immediately.

- Respond to the child's symptoms appropriately.

- Seek medical advice if you are uncertain about what to do, or if the child's condition causes prolonged pain or discomfort.

- If the child displays abnormal behaviors or symptoms as the result of an accident or injury, seek medical attention immediately.

- To help you identify common illnesses by their symptoms, buy a medical dictionary of children's illnesses.

Recognizing Mental Health Needs

- Observe and note when a child displays unusual emotional behavior such as extreme mood swings, excessive crying or fear, withdrawal, depression, or sudden loss of interest in friends and activities.

- Observe and note when a child exhibits extreme behaviors such as frequent and violent temper tantrums, head banging, or violence toward parents, siblings, or peers.

- Seek advice from the child's pediatrician to decide if counseling, therapy, or some other intervention is necessary.

- Ask the pediatrician for a referral to a mental health clinic, behavioral health pediatric clinic, or some other appropriate facility where you can take the child for assessment and treatment.

- Ask the pediatrician's office to help you make an appointment for your child to be evaluated by a mental or behavioral health professional.

Obtaining Medical or Mental Health Advice

- Look in the phone book for hotline numbers that offer free medical or mental health advice, and numbers for public health agencies and/or community clinics and hospitals.

- Think of helpful medical and mental health professionals you have used in the past.

- Ask friends, relatives, and trusted neighbors for the names and numbers of health care resources.

- Make a list of names and phone numbers of helpful health care professionals. Include emergency medical numbers such as 911, poison control numbers, a family counselor, and a number for a local pharmacist.

- Put the list where it is easy to find and read.

- When you think you may need medical advice, refer to the list to find the resource that might best be able to answer the question.

- When calling a health care professional, clearly explain the purpose of the call and the questions you have.

- Ask any questions you may have about the professional's explanations. Write down what he or she says.

- If the person is unable to answer your questions or give you the advice you need, ask him or her to refer you to someone who can help you.

- Listen to the advice and write down any referral numbers.

- Thank the person for helping you.

Choosing a Medical or Mental Health Professional or Facility

- Determine your medical care needs and concerns (a specific kind of doctor or medical specialist, a medical facility or mental health clinic that's close to home, services available, cost, and whether your insurance will be accepted).

- Check out available options by talking to friends, looking through the phone book, or asking a medical professional or health insurance agent for a referral.

- Choose two or three medical or mental health professionals or facilities that best fit your needs. Make a list, putting what appears to be the best option at the top.

- Contact the first professional's office and verify that it provides the services you need and meets any other criteria that are important to you.

- If you are not satisfied, contact the next office

on the list to see if it can provide the services you need.

- Find out where to go in case of a medical or mental health emergency and where to go for non-emergency care.

Keeping Medical or Mental Health Appointments

- Write down the time and location of the appointment on a calendar immediately after scheduling the appointment.

- Check the calendar daily.

- A couple of days in advance, call and confirm the day and time of the appointment.

- Arrange transportation, if necessary. (Medicaid or the U.S. Department of Health and Human Services may be able to provide you with a bus or subway pass, gas card, or cab fare to the appointment.)

- Gather any papers, records, or other items that you might need to take to the appointment (insurance card, birth certificate, money).

- Determine how long it will take to get to the appointment. Leave early and arrive for the appointment twenty minutes early.

- Notify the receptionist when you arrive for the appointment.

- If you are unable to keep an appointment for any reason, call as soon as possible to cancel and reschedule the appointment.

Understanding Health Insurance or Medicaid Coverage

- Read the information provided before you sign up for a health insurance plan or Medicaid coverage.

- Ask your employer's benefits office or the Medicaid office staff to answer any questions you have.

- Be sure you know what you need to do to remain eligible for the coverage you have.

- Know what your co-pays will be when you make a doctor's appointment.

- Keep information on hand on how to file a claim or how to dispute a denial of coverage.

Keeping Children Healthy

- When children are running a temperature or feeling sick, keep them home from school or day care. Arrange for babysitting if you must go to work.

- Follow treatment instructions from doctors.

- Complete giving all prescribed medications.

- Keep in touch with the doctor if your child's health is not improving.

- Keep a record of each child's illnesses, allergies, and any reactions to medications to share with doctors.

Administering Medication

- Ask the pharmacist and the physician or psychiatrist to explain how and when medication should be given.

- Obtain medication in a form that is age appropriate (liquid oral medication for younger children, pills or capsules for older children).

- Read the directions on the bottle and any directions that are provided by the doctor or the pharmacist.

- Ask the pharmacist about possible side effects of the medication and any special conditions that might apply (taking the medication with food, restrictions on certain activities).

- Plan your daily schedule around times when the medication is to be given.

- If the child needs medicine while in school or in child care, get the medicine and a complete set of instructions for using it to the school nurse or child-care provider.

- Give the medication as directed.

- With older children, make sure a child has taken the medication by asking the child or watching him or her take it.

- If a dose is missed, follow the instructions or call the pharmacist to find out what to do.

- Watch for and report any side effects to the doctor.

- If at any time questions arise about the medication, contact the doctor or the pharmacist immediately.

Keeping Track of Medications

- Make a list of medications and the times they are to be taken.

- Monitor when a medication is taken.

- On a calendar or log, write down the dosage and the time the medication was taken.

- Note on the calendar or log when medication is missed or taken late.

- List any unusual events, behaviors, or symptoms that are displayed by the child who is taking the medication.

- If a prescription needs to be refilled, get the refill a few days before the medication runs out so the child does not miss any doses.

- Provide information on when medications were taken or missed to a physician or health professional, if necessary.

- Store all medications out of the reach of children and follow all storage instructions. (Some medications need to be kept in a refrigerator.)

Getting a Child Immunized

- Contact a doctor, public health agency, or local school nurse to find out what immunizations your child needs.

- Decide where to take the child for immunizations (family doctor, local public health office).

- Find out how much each shot costs and whether medical benefits will cover all or part of the cost.

- Take all records of past immunizations with you each time you take the child for an immunization.

- When getting your child immunized, ask the health professional about any side effects or discomfort the child might experience.

- After the immunization, call the doctor immediately if your child has any unexpected reactions.

- Ask a medical professional to help you schedule immunizations for your child so they can be completed in a timely manner.

- Mark dates for future immunizations on the calendar.

- Update the child's personal medical records each time he or she is immunized.

- Review the calendar periodically in order to stay on schedule with the immunizations.

CHAPTER 9

Money Management

PROBLEM: The family has difficulty maintaining a budget or managing its money.

At some time or another, most families struggle with making ends meet. Commonly, people spend more money than their income allows, and for a time, find themselves in debt or unable to pay for things they need. Some people develop patterns of living beyond their means, are in a constant state of financial crisis, or may suddenly be laid off or fired from their jobs. Others make poor investments and find themselves so far in debt that they can not feasibly pay off their bills. When families experience financial problems, they may not be able to meet their children's basic needs. In extreme cases, children may not get adequate clothing, food, or shelter when their parents are unable to afford these items.

Money problems arise when parents don't have sufficient income, are unemployed or in debt, overspend, or spend their money on items they want rather than those that they need. Some families are simply victims of poverty and do not have the resources or income to buy the necessities. Regardless of the cause of a family's financial difficulties, parents, caregivers, and teens can all benefit from learning skills for improving money management and getting the financial assistance that is necessary to make ends meet. (Other chapters such as Nutrition and Informal and Formal Supports contain skills that are also helpful in this area. Check the Skills-at-a-Glance Table.)

Prioritizing

- List the basic daily needs of your children and yourself.

- List these needs in order of importance.

- Determine which needs your family can meet and which ones it needs help meeting.

- Review your list daily to make sure priority needs are being met.

- Meet the family's highest priority needs first.

Setting Up a Budget

- Determine a time span for the family budget (weekly, biweekly, or monthly).

- List all income sources and add up the family's total income.

- List all expenses and add up the total expenses. The expense list should include the cost of housing, utilities, child care, car payments, food, and the extras that are necessary to run a home.

- List debts that must be paid and add up the total amount.

- List non-necessity expenses that you would like to put in the budget; these could include recreation money, children's allowance, and personal savings.

- Subtract the expense total from the income total. If expenses are more than income, seek financial assistance to supplement the family income, or identify other ways of increasing income.

- If there is extra income, determine how much of each debt you can afford to pay while staying within the budget. Subtract that total from the remaining income amount.

- If any extra income remains, determine which non-necessity expense it will be used for in the budget.

- Consider your budget guidelines before spending money so that you can maintain the budget.

Monthly Budgeting

- List monthly expenses and income.

- List ways to obtain resources that can supplement income.

- Divide income, expenses, and other resources into four equal portions (one portion for each week of the month).

- Deposit an income allowance for each week into separate envelopes.

- Each week, pay expenses with the allowance from an envelope.

- If the weekly allowance does not cover expenses, use the additional resources for that week's expenses.

Applying for a Job

- Begin a job search by talking to family and friends, checking the newspaper classified ad section, career center, or job bank, and by doing a computer Internet search for "jobs" or "help wanted" with the name of your city and state to locate website listings of available jobs.

- Develop a professional-looking resume (strengths and past job experience listed, no spelling or grammatical errors, one page in length).

- Fill out all of the information requested on job applications truthfully.

- Prepare for a job interview by looking up information about the company, reading over the job position duties, and listing any questions you have.

- Practice appropriate interview skills – greeting someone, introducing yourself, making eye contact, maintaining good posture, listening, and saying "Thank you for the opportunity."

- Be properly groomed and attired for the interview – hair combed, clean and ironed clothes.

- After the interview, follow up with an e-mail, letter, or phone call, thanking the interviewer for his or her time and offering to answer any additional questions.

Opening a Checking Account

- Choose the financial institution where you want to bank. Ask about fees and special programs to help you make your decision.

- Take official identification, credit information, current account information, and money to deposit to the bank.

- Ask to talk with an account officer.

- Fill out an application and answer any questions.

- Choose the checking account plan that will best meet your needs.

- Ask about charges and penalties for overdrafts and using the account.

- Read and save all information about the account.

Saving Money

- Determine how much money from your budget can be put into savings.

- Choose the financial institution where you want to bank. Ask about fees and special programs to help you make your decision.

- Check out savings account options that will yield the best interest.

- Choose a savings plan.

- Deposit money into the savings account on a regular basis.

Paying a Bill

- Plan your budget so you will be able to pay bills.

- When you receive a bill, write a check or obtain a money order for the amount, and put it in an envelope with whatever paperwork must be returned with the payment.

- Address the envelope and put a stamp on it.

- Write the amount paid and the date the bill was mailed on the bill receipt.

- Save the receipt.

- Mail the bill at least three to five working days before it is due to avoid late fees. Consider delivering the payment in person to local companies if it is more convenient.

- Some monthly, regular bills (such as telephone, utilities, etc.) can be set up for automatic withdrawal from your checking account. If you set up such payments, write out the schedule of withdrawals and transfer them to your checking account on the due dates.

- If you have a computer and Internet connection, consider online bill paying to save money on checks and postage and reduce late payments.

Making a Late Payment

- Contact the company or creditor and explain that you will be unable to make the payment on time.

- Ask the creditor if special arrangements can be made for making a late payment.

- Ask if there will be a service charge and what that charge will be.

- Agree upon a late payment schedule that you can follow.

- Ask for a written agreement and get a copy.

- Thank the creditor for his or her time and assistance.

- Send in the late payment according to the plan you agree on.

Paying Off a Debt

- Find out the total amount of the debt, including interest.

- Ask the creditor for the minimum payment that will be accepted, and how much money you can save by paying off the debt early.

- Include in your budget at least a minimum regular payment to the creditor.

- Continue to make payments until the debt is completely paid.

- Keep receipts of all payments that are made.

- Save paperwork that shows that the debt was paid in full.

Shopping for Bargains

- List the items you need.

- Check ads and look for sales on those items.

- Save and use coupons for the items you need.

- Determine which stores have the best prices on the items.

- Consider shopping at flea markets, garage sales, thrift stores, and food co-ops instead of retail stores.

- Consider purchasing cheaper brands or second-hand goods (clothes, furniture, etc.). In retail stores, look for clearance items.

- Purchase only those items on the list.

- If you find a good sale on an item that is not on the list, decide if you'll need the item in the future and whether you should buy it now at the discount price.

Accessing Public Assistance and Other Available Resources

- Identify a problem for which you will need resources (unemployment benefits, food or food stamps, subsidized housing, transportation, health care, etc.).

- Find out what resources might be available by asking friends, relatives, and specialists, or checking in phone books, newspapers, the library, or online.

- List the resources that might be able help solve the problem.

- Contact places that can supply resources ahead of time to see how they can help and what you have to do to qualify or obtain the help.

- Ask about restrictions or limits on using the resource (resource can be used only once a month, dollar limit, or one-time only policy).

- Put the list of resource numbers where you can easily find it.

Using a Food Pantry

- Make a list of area food pantries; include their addresses and phone numbers.

- Call or visit a food pantry and ask about its rules.

- Use the food pantry when necessary and follow the rules.

- Ask pantry workers if they know of other area food resources that are available.

Understanding and Using Credit Appropriately

- Pay bills promptly to avoid late fees and to keep finance charges to a minimum.

- Shop for the best interest rates on credit cards or a loan if needed.

- Avoid borrowing money at excessively high interest rates on payday or other predatory loans.

- Avoid rent-to-own furniture and shop for affordable furnishings at garage sales and thrift stores.

- Never pay an advance fee to get a loan.

- To make purchases, use cash or a debit card that takes money directly out of your checking account instead of a credit card.

- Keep a file of your debit and credit card receipts to compare to your monthly statements.

- If you have a credit card balance, pay more than the minimum monthly balance to decrease the amount of time it will take to pay if off and the total amount of money you will pay.

- Try to put ten percent of your take-home pay toward debt payment. When your debts are paid off, put that money into savings.

- Check your credit report score several times a year (for free) by going to **annualcreditreport.com** or call (toll-free) 1-877-322-8228 to get the forms by mail.

Being a Wise Consumer

- Do not give your Social Security number and personal information to anyone you do not know.

- Check to see if the local United Way offers a free tax preparation service.

- Read contracts thoroughly and be sure you understand all terms. Be sure all oral promises are written down. Ask questions. Remember that three-day cancellations only apply to door-to-door and off-premise sale contracts.

- Do not update account information through an e-mail; legitimate companies will never ask you to do this.

- Shred personal mail and credit card offers. Sometimes companies offer free shredding services to the community.

- Be wary of consumer scams: never pay a fee to collect a "prize" or get information about a "work at home" scheme; don't pay for repairs or service before the work has been done; be wary of door-to door salesmen or repairmen; check with the Better Business Bureau or the state attorney general's office before hiring anyone for major service work.

- Remember that offers which sound "too good to be true," usually are.

CHAPTER 10

Child Supervision

PROBLEM: Children's activities are not being adequately monitored.

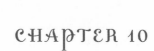

Monitoring children's activities means knowing where children are, who they are with, what they are doing, and when they will be home. It also involves teaching children about the risks they may face when they participate in certain activities, and being prepared to protect them from danger. Depending on the child's age, a parent or caregiver can teach a child what situations are okay and which ones should be avoided.

Children who do not receive appropriate supervision are at risk of encountering dangerous situations that they are unable to handle because they lack good judgment or maturity. Young children often can't or don't recognize that some activities can be dangerous. When they are not monitored, they are more likely to be victimized (sexual or physical abuse), suffer injury (accidents), get lost or be abducted, or not get their basic needs met. Teenagers who are not appropriately monitored are more likely to engage in delinquent behaviors, drug use, and sexual

75

behavior. Without proper supervision, children are denied the social and emotional attention that is necessary for healthy development.

Parents who provide adequate supervision are able to reduce the number of dangerous situations their children might encounter and teach their children how to get their needs met. A parent who monitors a child's activities knows when the child needs direction or help in avoiding hazards in the living environment. Monitoring young children requires parents to constantly be on guard for potential dangers, and to respond quickly if the children are putting themselves at risk. Prevention is the best way a parent can protect a child from harm. Here are some ways parents and caregivers can be more protective and keep their children safe.

Monitoring a Child's Whereabouts (Older Children)

- Set specific rules regarding where children can go, both inside and outside the home.

- Set specific expectations for the child's behavior when he or she is at a friend's home without adult supervision.

- Ask children where they are going before they leave the home.

- Teach children to report where they are going.

- Check regularly to make sure children are where they are supposed to be.

- Have the child let you know where he or she is on a regular basis.

- Respond with consequences if the child is not where he or she is supposed to be.

Pre-Approving a Child's Friends or Places to Go

- When the child asks to go to a friend's home or a place that you know little about, ask the child to tell you everything he or she knows about the friend or the place.

- Ask the child what he or she plans to do and when he or she plans to return.

- Call or visit the friend's home or the place.

- Talk to the friend's parent or the manager of the place to determine if the visit will be appropriate and safe for the child.

- Write down a phone number for where the child can be reached in case of an emergency.

- Before allowing the child to go, establish guidelines you want him or her to follow while at the place or friend's home.

- Get to know your child's friends when you can so you are aware of their personalities, values, and family situations. If possible, introduce yourself to the friends' parents.

Monitoring a Child's Activities (Younger Children)

- Check every room in the home and remove or fix any potential hazards before allowing children in the room (sharp objects, matches or lighters, uncovered electrical outlets, mousetraps, poisons, etc.). Check outside play areas as well.

- When a child is awake, keep him or her in a place where you can easily see the child.

- Frequently check to make sure the child is not in any dangerous situations.

- If the child goes out of sight, return the child to a more visible location or move closer to where the child is.

- Remove the child from potentially dangerous situations, and redirect his or her attention to something else.

- Teach the child about potential dangers (hot stove, electrical outlets, crossing the street, etc.).

- When a child is in bed, periodically check to make sure that he or she remains in bed.

CHILD SUPERVISION

Asking about a Child's Activities

- When a child returns from an activity, ask the adult who was in charge how the child behaved and what occurred.

- Ask the child how he or she behaved and what he or she did.

- Determine whether the activity and the child's behavior were acceptable, and decide if you will let the child do this activity again.

Monitoring an Infant

- Sit or lay an infant in locations that are clean, dry, and free of dangerous objects. (Any small item an infant can put in his or her mouth is potentially dangerous.)

- If an infant cannot yet sit up, make sure the child's back, neck, and head are supported.

- Secure padding around hard surfaces (crib railings, floors, walls, table corners, etc.) that an infant may roll or fall against.

- Never leave an infant unattended on a high surface like a couch, chair, bed, or changing table. Also, never leave an infant alone in a bathtub or sink, or near water (swimming or wading pool, bucket, pond, lake, etc.).

- Always make sure the infant is in a location where you can fully see and hear him or her.

- Frequently look at the infant to make sure he or she is okay.

- If an infant appears to be chewing or sucking, check his or her mouth for foreign objects.

Baby Proofing Your Home

- Clear table and counter surfaces below your chest level.

- Install magnetic cabinet and drawer locks.

- Place plug covers over electrical outlets.

- Install gates in doorways and at the top and bottom of stairs.

- Put a deadbolt lock or chain at the top of exterior doors.

- For more advice on steps to take to make your home safe for babies and toddlers, do an Internet search for "baby proofing."

Finding Child Care

- List ways to locate child-care providers, such as looking in the phone book, asking friends and neighbors, or looking in the newspaper.

- Make a large list of child-care providers.

- Select three candidates to interview.

- Write down a list of questions to ask the candidates. Ask about things like the type of discipline the provider uses, experience in caring for children, hours, rules, fees, and meals and snacks.

- Contact and interview each candidate.

- Get references from the provider, including names and phone numbers of families the provider is serving or has served.

- Contact and interview the reference families.

- If the child-care provider is licensed, contact the local licensing board to ask about the quality of the facility.

- Choose the provider who will best fit your needs.

- Take your child to meet the provider.

- If you are satisfied with how the meeting goes, set a starting date for child care.

- If you are not satisfied with the outcome of the child's first meeting with the provider, choose

CHILD SUPERVISION

another candidate and repeat the interview process.

Communicating with Your Child's Caregiver

- Prepare for a meeting with your child's caregiver by writing down what you want to say and what questions you want to ask.

- Think about how to state your concerns in a positive manner.

- Call ahead and schedule an appointment with the caregiver.

- Stay calm and positive throughout the conversation. Avoid blaming or becoming defensive.

- Be open to and supportive of the caregiver's suggestions.

- If you are having discipline problems with your child, ask for the caregiver's advice and support.

Hiring a Babysitter

- Ask friends, neighbors, or relatives for recommendations for babysitters.

- Make a list of all potential babysitters.

- Contact and interview each prospective baby sitter. Discuss the babysitter's experience, fees, references, etc.

- Select two or three babysitters you can call whenever you need someone to stay with your child.

- Have the babysitter meet your child before you hire the sitter.

- Determine if the babysitter will come to your home, or if you need to take the child to the sitter's home. (If the child will be watched in the babysitter's home, visit the home ahead of time to make sure it is safe and clean.)

- Schedule the babysitter as far in advance as possible.

- Invite the sitter to come to your home twenty minutes before you have to leave so you can review house rules, show the sitter around the home, discuss how the child should be disciplined, explain what food is available for the child and sitter, and go over information about where you will be, when you will return, and how you can be contacted in case of an emergency.

- Leave the sitter a list of important phone numbers (doctor, poison control, relatives, etc.).

- Talk to your child about the rules for behavior when the babysitter is providing care.

- When you return home, ask the babysitter for a full update on the child's behavior and the activities of the night.

- Talk to your child about the babysitter. Ask your child if the sitter was fair, protective, pleasant, and attentive.

- If you have an older child who you trust is capable of watching your younger children, enroll the child in a babysitting class first. Many American Red Cross and 4-H Chapters offer such classes for eleven- to fifteen-year-olds.

- Consider joining or starting a babysitting cooperative with other parents you know through the neighborhood, school, or church. Information and tips on forming a cooperative are available online.

Transporting Children in a Car

- Determine if the vehicle will safely hold the number of children you need to transport.

- Children should not sit in the front seat of a car with an airbag.

- Remove hazardous objects from the area where the children will be sitting.

CHILD SUPERVISION

- Secure all car seats and/or booster seats that you may need in the car according to instructions. Safety experts recommend that car seats be secured in the back seat of a vehicle. Many communities have safety fairs where you can go to be sure seats are safely installed.

- Children who weigh under forty pounds should be secured in an infant car seat. (If a child weighs under twenty pounds, the infant car seat should face the rear of the car.)

- Children who are between ages four and eight and less than four feet nine inches tall should be secured in a booster seat.

- All children who do not need to be in a car seat or booster seat should wear a seat belt.

- Make sure that children's hands and feet are clear of the doors and windows before closing them.

- Make sure that all the children are safely buckled in their seats before starting the car.

- Give the children appropriate toys or items to keep them occupied while you are driving.

- If you need to attend to the children for any reason while driving, pull over and park the car in a safe location first.

- Occasionally check to see that the children are sitting properly and are safely buckled in their seats.

- When getting out of the car, have the children remain in their seats until the engine is off and you are ready to monitor their exit. Never leave children unattended in a vehicle.

CHAPTER 11

Informal and Formal Support

PROBLEM: The family is socially isolated and lacks support from others.

Social isolation occurs when a family is separated from relatives, friends, and helping persons. There are many reasons why a family may be isolated. Living in a rural setting, suspicion of strangers, lack of social skills, language or cultural barriers, and a preference for being self-reliant all are factors that can contribute to isolation. Even people who associate with many people may lack social support if those relationships are not healthy, durable, and balanced. When a family is isolated, it suffers in times of crisis because its resources for support are limited.

Help during stressful times often comes in the form of informal support, advice, and encouragement from persons

85

outside the immediate family system. Relationships with others provide family members with more opportunities to learn and be involved in a variety of activities. Children benefit when their families are socially connected with others such as neighbors, friends, relatives, parents of classmates, church members, etc. Other adults can provide additional role-modeling and extra protection as they join with the family in looking out for the child's welfare. Other people can help the family meet concrete needs, too. Outside relationships often yield offers of assistance in areas like child care, transportation, finances, and home maintenance.

In addition, there are many formal support systems that are available to help adults and children find assistance from a group of peers or mentors. Examples include Parents without Partners for single parents, Alcoholics Anonymous, Alanon and Alateen for families impacted by substance abuse, Lamplighters for parents of a child who has died, Parents Anonymous which helps parents who have abused their children, Boys and Girls Clubs for children who need healthy social and recreational activities, and Big Brothers and Big Sisters for children in need of an adult role model. These are just a few of the many formal support groups that exist for families in need. Practitioners can help them locate appropriate local groups based on the needs and interests of parents and children.

Some of the skills people can learn to help them establish healthy social support networks and find formal support groups are listed here.

Making Friends

- Identify someone you would like to meet.
- Call the person or meet with him or her in the community.
- Start a conversation by introducing yourself.
- Talk with the person, sharing information about each other.
- Ask the person about his or her interests.
- Identify common interests and talk more about these.

- Tell the person that you would like to talk again in the future.

- Ask the person if he or she would like to talk with you again.

- If the person is interested, contact him or her on a regular basis to talk.

- Plan an activity with the person.

Establishing Relationship Boundaries

- Decide what kind of information, help, or friendship you are willing to offer to or accept from another person. These limits or rules that define what you want in a relationship are your boundaries.

- Let the other person know that you feel uncomfortable if he or she crosses one of your boundaries.

- If the person will not respect your boundaries, consider ending the relationship.

- Stick to any boundaries you set for the relationship.

Deciding Who to Ask for Help

- Determine what you need.

- Think about who could help you meet your need.

- Decide whether it would be better to ask a professional, a stranger, a relative, or a friend to help with the problem.

- Choose the person who would be most available and capable to help.

- Consider the advantages and disadvantages of asking that person for help. (Will that person charge you for the help? Is that person likely to expect a bigger favor in return?)

- Determine if you have something you could exchange for the help you need.

- In a clear, straightforward manner, state what you need and ask for help.

- If that person is not able to help, choose another person.

Offering Help

- Look for opportunities to help someone.

- Ask the person if he or she would like help.

- Listen to what the person would like from you.

- Offer help you know you can provide.

- Follow through with what you agree to do for the person.

- Check back to see if there is anything else you can do to help.

Developing a Social Support Network

- List all the people you come into contact with in an average week.

- Decide whether these people are friends, professional acquaintances, relatives, or people you just know.

- For each person listed, decide if the relationship is balanced or if one person gives more while the other person receives more.

- Determine if any of these relationships are unhealthy because you have to give too much and receive little support in return.

- Build relationships with people who have a good balance of give and take with you.

- Decide which areas of your life need more support (financial, emotional, spiritual, or physical).

- Determine if you are relying too heavily on any one person to help you meet your needs.

- Develop healthy relationships with people who have positive lifestyles and can be supportive.

- Consider joining a social group (bowling league, Bible study, parent support group) to meet more people.

Setting Up Exchange Systems (Cooperative Borrowing)

- Identify tasks you need help with or items that you need to borrow.

- Think about people in your community (neighbors, church members, your child's classmates' parents) who may have what you need or could help you.

- List goods and services you could offer in exchange for things you would borrow from others.

- Approach the person with whom you would like to set up an exchange.

- Ask the person if he or she would be willing to trade goods or services (offer to watch the person's child after school in exchange for using his or her phone occasionally).

- Talk with the person about the guidelines for the trade. (When is it okay to use the phone?)

Getting Involved in Community Activities

- Look for opportunities to volunteer for community projects (read newspapers, school newsletters, and bulletin board postings in the library or laundromat).

- Consider all the options for community activities.

- Weigh the advantages and disadvantages of each option.

- Decide which activity you would like to do.

- Contact the leader or coordinator of the community activity.

- Explain why you are interested in the activity.

- Ask how you can get involved.

- Tell the person how you would like to help.

SUPPORT

- Ask how and when you can get started.

- Be prepared to make a time commitment to the activity.

- Follow through with whatever offer of help or participation you make.

Finding a Support Group

- Assess areas of your life where you or your children are having problems. (Do you or your children have a substance abuse issue with alcohol or drugs? Are you going through a divorce? Do you have a medical or mental health problem you are having trouble coping with? Do you need to lose weight? Do your children need a safe and healthy place to meet friends and play?)

- Ask professionals who you deal with (for example, a doctor, nurse, counselor, pastor, etc.) for any information he or she has about a recommended support group you might join.

- Get information about appropriate support groups by looking in the telephone directory under "Support Groups" or go online and do a search for "(problem) support groups (your city or town and state)."

- Call the support group and ask questions about its activities, members, meeting times and places, and how to join.

- Ask if you may attend a meeting to learn more before formally joining the group.

- After attending, think about whether you felt comfortable with the group, liked the members you met, and believe the group can benefit you or your children.

- If you decide to join the support group, commit to regularly attending, participating, and using its discussions and activities to help you better deal with your problem.

CHAPTER 12

Nutrition

PROBLEM: Children's nutritional needs are not being adequately met.

Understanding the nutritional needs and providing proper diets for children is a difficult and time-consuming process for most families. When parents have stressful or demanding work schedules, or when children are picky eaters or groceries are expensive, planning and preparing well-rounded meals can be a challenge. Parents and caregivers must know what foods are healthy and appropriate for children. They also need to know how to coordinate the buying, cooking, and storing of foods. Unfortunately, when parents or caregivers don't know what foods a child needs or how to prepare them, a child's health may be endangered. In some cases, the result can be severe malnutrition requiring medical intervention. To promote healthy growth and development, families often can learn basic skills for consistently meeting a child's nutritional needs. The following skills are related to nutrition and establishing healthy eating habits for families.

Creating a Balanced Menu

- List the food groups that should be represented on the menu. (Contact the public health department, county extension agent, school nurse, a doctor, or a nutritional specialist for nutritional guidelines.)

- For each group, make a list of foods the family likes, knows how to prepare, and can afford.

- Create meals that include each of the necessary food groups, including fruits and vegetables.

- Make several variations of balanced menus.

- Include typical meals for breakfast, lunch, and supper on the menus.

- Include healthy beverages on the menus.

- Store menus until they are needed for meal planning.

Planning Ahead for Meals

- Choose meal menus that are balanced and nutritious.

- Make a list of foods that are needed to make each meal.

- Buy the food on the list.

- Properly store food items until you need them.

- Set regular mealtimes.

- Prepare the menu items prior to the established mealtime.

Choosing Appropriate Foods for Babies and Toddlers

- Talk with your doctor regularly about your child's special dietary needs.

- Follow the doctor's instructions on what foods the child can and should eat.

- Serve nutritious foods the child likes. Don't force the child to eat.

- Introduce your child to new foods several times before abandoning them if the child doesn't like the foods.

- At mealtime, provide each child with a serving that is appropriate for his or her size and age.

- Cut and serve solid foods into small pieces that a child can easily chew without choking.

- If child is eating more or less than what the doctor has recommended, consult with the doctor again.

Shopping for Groceries

- Before going to the store, make a list of all the grocery items you need to buy.

- Collect any coupons you have for the items on your list.

- Figure out about how much the groceries will cost and take enough money to pay for them.

- Choose a grocery store that will carry most or all of the items on your list at the best price.

- Do not go to the store hungry. (People sometimes buy much more than they need or can use.)

- If you have many items on your list, get a shopping cart as you enter the store.

- Begin at one end of the store, and walk up and down each aisle picking out the items on your list.

- If there are two or more brands of the item you want, compare the size and prices, and choose the one that is the best value and fits your needs. It generally costs less to buy items in bulk, but you should determine whether you will be able to use up the item before it spoils.

- Check off each item on your list as you pick up the item.

- Keep a running total of the cost of your groceries by writing down prices or adding them on a calculator as you shop. This will help you stay within your budget.

- If buying frozen foods, pick out those items last so they are more likely to stay frozen on your way home.

- When you have all the items on your grocery list, proceed to the checkout line.

- Give the cashier any coupons you have for items you are buying.

- Allow the cashier to price all the items and tell you the total.

- Pay the cashier.

- Take the bagged groceries and receipt home with you.

Preparing a Meal

- Decide in advance what meal to prepare.

- Read through the recipe or instructions if you are unfamiliar with how to prepare the meal.

- Make sure all of the necessary ingredients are available.

- Thaw frozen items in the refrigerator in advance.

- Set out all necessary ingredients and cooking utensils.

- Determine appropriate cooking, baking, and/or chilling times.

- Allow enough time to cook food items so they will be done by mealtime.

- Serve the meal at the established mealtime.

Storing Food

- When buying food, note if it needs to be refrigerated or kept frozen.

- Follow storage instructions that are written on refrigerated and frozen food packages. Do not refreeze uncooked meat once it has thawed.

- Cover and refrigerate leftover foods immediately. Put a piece of masking tape on containers and write the date so you'll know how old leftovers are.

- Before preparing food that has been stored, smell it to make sure it's not spoiled. Do not eat discolored or foul-smelling food.

- Note the freshness or expiration date on perishable food items, and throw away food that is older than the date.

- Cover and seal dry goods after they have been opened.

- Keep food in sealed containers so that pets and pests cannot get to it.

- Store food away from toxic chemicals such as bleach or other cleaners.

Washing Dishes

- Gather all the dirty dishes that need to be washed.

- Scrape food residue off the dishes into the trash or garbage disposal.

- Put dishwashing soap in the sink and fill it with hot water.

- Soak the dishes in the hot water for a few minutes.

- Wash the dishes using a dish rag or pan scrubber. Wipe the entire surface of each dish at least once, and continue wiping until the surface is free of food residue.

- Rinse off each dish in hot water.

- Place clean dishes in a draining rack so that water will run off them.

- Dry the dishes with a clean dish towel.

- Store the dishes in a cupboard.

CHAPTER 13

Preventing Abuse

PROBLEM: Children are not safe from physical, emotional, and/or sexual abuse. A parent is threatened with or is the victim of domestic violence.

Abuse of children can take many different forms – physical, emotional, and sexual. Punching, slapping, spanking and other violence can leave psychological as well as physical scars on children. Emotional types of abuse including name-calling, belittling, and constant criticism can batter children's self-esteem and threaten their well-being and healthy development.

Sexual abuse, by its very nature, is a secretive activity that often is veiled in lies, threats, and manipulation. A child who has been sexually abused in the past is at a greater risk of being victimized again than a child who has not been sexually abused. A child who has not been victimized, but who is living in a home situation where a perpetrator (the person who committed the abusive act) could take advantage of the child, also is threatened. Sometimes, the children at highest risk are those who are not adequately protected by a parent or caregiver. The parent may not be aware of the dangers, or may be in denial about the potential for abuse. Though denial is a very common reaction when family members learn that sexual abuse is occurring, counseling can help them to acknowledge that it did happen and can happen again.

Domestic violence is a pattern of abuse where one person exercises control over another through threats and intimidation, physical and sexual violence, emotional abuse, isolation, or economic deprivation. It can happen whether couples are married, living together, or dating and may be life-threatening to its victim.

Once abuse is discovered or domestic violence is acknowledged, it may take a great deal of time to resolve the related issues. Families sometimes require therapy to deal with the emotional impact of abuse, especially sexual abuse. Victims of domestic violence and their children may have to find a safe way to escape from the abuser's control. Many skills can be taught to parents and caregivers that will enable them to prevent further abuse and protect their children. Some of those skills are presented here.

Understanding and Avoiding Physical Abuse of Children

- Discuss what constitutes physical abuse with your family consultant/practitioner.

- Assess your (and your partner's) relationship with your children: Do either of you ever hit, slap, shake, pinch, or otherwise physically harm your children?

- Assess your children's physical well-being: Do they ever have bruises or other physical injuries that they will not or cannot explain? Are there adults or other children they avoid or do not want to be left alone with?

- Identify your "hot" buttons – which behaviors of your children or events in your life trigger your anger?

- Write down a list of nonviolent ways that could help you cope with those hot buttons and stay calm – calling a friend, taking a walk, deep breathing, washing your face with cool water, asking a trustworthy relative or friend to watch your child for a while.

- Create a plan for how you will keep your children safe if you feel they are threatened with physical violence from you, your partner, or anyone else.

- Identify another family member or friend who could take and safely supervise your children in an emergency and talk to him or her about how and when you might ask for such assistance.

Understanding and Avoiding Emotional Abuse of Children

- Discuss what constitutes emotional abuse with your family consultant/practitioner.

- Assess your (and your partner's) relationship with your children: Do you engage in screaming, name-calling, threatening, blaming, accusing, or excessive criticizing of your children?

- Recognize what circumstances or behaviors trigger your anger.

- Balance criticism with praise by looking for the good things your children do and complimenting those behaviors often.

- Don't expect your children's behavior to be "perfect:" Set reasonable expectations for them based on their age and abilities.

- Recognize your children's need to be loved, nurtured, touched, and accepted by you.

- Write down a plan for how you will calm down and stay in control when you have to deal with your children in an emotional situation.

- Identify another family member or friend who could take and safely supervise your children when you feel your emotions are out of control and you need a break.

- If you do lose control and say something to your child that you regret, apologize and say what you will do differently in the future.

- Consider taking a parenting class to learn effective methods of self-control and discipline.

Teaching Children about Appropriate Touch

- Prepare for the discussion by getting information about personal body safety and how to discuss sensitive issues. Look for resources at the library, school, child welfare office, or public health department.

- Choose a time and place that is convenient and safe for you and the child.

- Talk about the child's body and his or her right to protect it from others.

- Describe what parts of the body are private (the parts covered by a swimsuit).

- Explain the difference between acceptable and unacceptable touches from others.

- Set clear boundaries for what is appropriate touch and inappropriate touch in your family.

- Tell the child how he or she should respond if someone uses inappropriate touch.

- Answer or clarify any questions the child may have.

- Listen and respond accordingly if the child chooses to disclose any information about being inappropriately touched.

- Occasionally, review the issue of appropriate touch with the child.

Setting Boundaries

- Explain what personal boundaries are and why they are necessary. Personal boundaries are the limits people set to protect their bodies and belongings from others. A person's boundaries determine how close others can come to that person, and give people the right to keep others from touching them, taking something from them, or invading their privacy without permission.

- Define what types of activities would be appropriate and what activities would violate personal boundaries.

- Set clear rules for respecting other people's boundaries regarding the body and personal belongings. For example, set rules for when and where to get dressed, bathing, using appropriate language, borrowing clothes, and touching others.

- Explain that it is okay for a child to say "No" if another child or adult tries to violate his or her personal boundaries.

- Explain the consequences for breaking the rules and violating someone's personal boundaries.

- Help your child maintain boundaries by not allowing relatives and friends to force physical affection (hugs, kisses) on the child if he or she doesn't want them to.

Monitoring Children in the Presence of a Potential Perpetrator

- Set clear boundaries for the child ahead of time. Consider boundaries for hugs or touches, staying in sight of a safe adult, and appropriate conversation.

- Stand or sit where you can see and hear any interactions between the child and the potential perpetrator.

- Take action if the child or the perpetrator crosses any boundary that may pose a danger to the child.

- After a visit, ask the child if there was a time when the potential perpetrator made him or her feel unsafe or uncomfortable. If so, respond accordingly.

Locating Registered Sex Offenders

- On a home or library computer, go to a website such as the Department of Justice National/State Sex Offender Registry at **fbi.gov/hq/cid/cac/registry.htm** or **familywatchdog.us** and do a search of the registry using your state, address, and zip code.

- Note the addresses of registered sex offenders in your neighborhood and other areas frequented by your children.

- Make a plan to keep your children away from the area around an offender's residence or make sure children are accompanied by an adult when in the vicinity.

- Check with the local police about what additional steps you should take to protect your children.

Asking Children about Personal Safety

- Choose a convenient time for you and the child to talk.

- Choose a place where the conversation cannot be overheard by others.

- Ask the child if he or she ever feels unsafe, has been touched inappropriately, or has been physically harmed by someone else.

- If the child is bruised or shows signs of other physical injury, ask how he or she was injured.

- Give the child examples of different kinds of unsafe situations to make sure he or she understands what types of situations you are asking about.

- Explain the difference between appropriate and inappropriate touches.

- Listen to the child.

- Ask questions to get more information if the child talks about feeling unsafe, being touched inappropriately, or being abused.

- Respond to any of the child's disclosures with openness and acceptance. Do not get defensive or make the child feel that he or she is to blame.

- Thank the child for being willing to talk with you.

- Encourage the child to come to you any time he or she feels unsafe or anytime someone harms him or her. Convey to the child that you want to keep him or her safe.

- Occasionally ask the child about her or his sense of personal safety.

Responding to a Child's Disclosure about Abuse

- If child discloses any information about current or past sexual or physical abuse, take time to listen to what the child is saying.

- Arrange to talk with the child in a safe and comfortable location.

- Assure the child that you can be trusted and that you will protect him or her from future harm.

- Tell the child the abuse was not his or her fault, and that he or she did the right thing in telling you.

- To the extent that the child is willing and able to talk, ask the child questions about the incident(s). Find out who was involved, and where and when the incident(s) occurred.

- Listen to the child's account with acceptance and reassurance. Avoid making statements that might make the child feel responsible or at fault for what has happened.

- Make a plan for keeping the child away from the accused perpetrator.

- Determine whether the police should be notified immediately. If so, call the police.

- Seek advice and support from a professional to find out what else you should do to protect your child (contact a therapist, family doctor, school counselor, and/or child protective services).

Reporting Abuse

- Listen, without judgment, when a child wants to talk about any inappropriate touch, sexual advance, or physical assault made by another person. With young children, look for any physical signs that might indicate that the child has been sexually or physically abused.

- Ask questions to help you determine and understand when, where, and how the abuse occurred, and who was involved.

- Contact the appropriate authorities immediately; this could be a therapist, child protective services, and/or the police.

- With the help of the authorities, determine if the child needs immediate medical attention or a medical exam.

Seeking Support When Dealing with Abuse

- Check out options for obtaining help or support. Check whether these options are available: sexual or physical abuse survivors' groups, counseling, a trusted friend who will respond without judgment, and/or a religious leader.

- Decide with whom you would feel most comfortable and confident discussing the abuse.

- Talk with the person.

- Choose more than one person to talk with, if necessary.

Establishing a Safety Plan

- Choose a safe place and a convenient time for you and the child to talk.

- Discuss the importance of protecting oneself and having a plan if someone makes a person feel unsafe.

- Tell the child what he or she should do if he or she feels unsafe. This can include yelling for help, running away, immediately telling a trusted adult what happened, never keeping secrets, and not talking to strangers.

- Decide on a special "password" the child can use to tell you that he or she needs help immediately without someone else knowing.

- Practice the safety plan to make sure the child knows what to do.

- Occasionally check with the child to make sure he or she remembers the safety plan.

Understanding Domestic Violence

- Understand that physical violence is never an appropriate response to problems between spouses, partners, or parents and children, and that the recipient of the assault should not be "blamed" for the violence.

- Understand that children are damaged from witnessing physical violence in the home even if they are not assaulted themselves.

- Any spouse or partner with anger or violence issues should be encouraged to seek counseling to learn how to release anger and solve problems nonviolently.

- Learn about the cycle of domestic violence by going to the website, **domesticviolence.org**, and download the violence chart.

- Understand that an abuser may deny the abuse, blame the victim, promise never to abuse again, give gifts, etc., but the cycle can occur hundreds of times in an abusive relationship.

Responding to Domestic Violence

- If you are in an abusive relationship, develop a personalized safety plan: collect emergency numbers and program them on your cell phone, ask neighbors to call the police if they hear angry or violent noises, teach children to call 911, plan and practice ways to get out of the house, gather things you might need in an emergency (money, keys, important papers, extra clothes for you and the children, etc.,) and store them in a private location outside the home.

• If you or your children have been or are in imminent danger of being physically assaulted, call 911 for police assistance.

• If you and your children need a safe place (shelter) to go to escape or avoid domestic violence, call the police, a local hotline, or the National Domestic Violence Hotline at 1-800-799-SAFE (7233).

• Contact an attorney or a local legal aid society if you wish to seek a personal protection order or restraining order against an abuser.

• If you decide to leave an abusive relationship or if the abuser has already left, plan carefully for the safety of you and your children. Consult with your family consultant/practitioner, a counselor, or a specialist at a domestic violence hotline to help you create your plan.

CHAPTER 14

Managing Stress

PROBLEM: A family member has difficulty dealing with stress.

Stress can sometimes seem overwhelming and difficult to endure. Everyone faces stress, but when people become overwhelmed by it, they are generally expecting too much of themselves and others. This can lead to disappointment, worry, and frustration. When people are under high stress, they often are at a greater risk of reacting in desperate ways. Decisions made under stress are frequently irrational or impulsive, and can have negative results. Child abuse, domestic violence, self-injury, and depression sometimes occur because a person is unable to effectively cope with stress.

Because stress is a fact of life, family members must learn how to manage it, rather than to rid themselves of it. Some people may require counseling and/or medical care when it becomes difficult for them to function normally; many benefit from the support and encouragement that comes from professional help. People also can learn coping skills, which can improve family life and help them regain a sense of control in their personal lives. Here are a few skills that are effective for managing stress.

Managing Time *

- List everything you want to accomplish during a set time period.

- Estimate the time it will take to complete each task.

- Give important tasks top priority.

- Allow extra time for delays and setbacks.

- Make a schedule for completing each task.

- Be sure to include breaks and time for relaxation activities.

- Evaluate and revise the schedule if you find that you are unable to keep up with it.

Recognizing Stressors

- Think back to the last few times you felt overwhelmed by stress.

- Identify what was happening and what you were thinking and feeling just before you felt the stress.

- Write down any common themes in the events, thoughts, or feelings that usually accompany feelings of stress. These are your stress indicators, or stressors.

- Note when these indicators occur again.

- The next several times you experience stress, write down the details of the situation to become better aware of when stressors are occurring.

- Prepare yourself by using relaxation techniques or self-talk. (These will be explained later.)

Engaging in Self-Care Activities

- List activities you enjoy that you associate with feeling calm and relaxed.

- Order the activities according to how easy and accessible they are.

- Schedule a regular time to do an activity you enjoy.

- If you encounter many stressful situations, take time out to do a relaxing activity.

- Remind yourself that it is important to care for your own needs so that you can deal with the needs of others.

Choosing Relaxation Techniques

- Consider a variety of ways to relax; for example, deep-breathing, counting to ten, working on a hobby, talking with a friend, or writing in a journal.

- Practice new relaxation techniques so you will have a variety of techniques to choose from.

- Decide which techniques are easiest and help you relax the most.

- When facing a stressful situation, pick a relaxation technique to engage in.

Getting Physically Active

- Increase the amount of exercise you and your children get to at least thirty minutes of brisk activity three to five times each week.

- Locate parks, playgrounds, recreation centers, public swimming pools, YMCA/YWCAs, Boys and Girls Clubs, or other facilities that offer no- or low-cost recreational programs and encourage family members to participate.

- Find activities you can do as a family – for example, walking, jogging, swimming, bicycling, pickup basketball or volleyball games.

- Find fitness programs on television or borrow DVDs from the library that give you an exercise routine to follow at home.

Taking a Time-Out

- Notice when you begin to feel physical indicators of stress.

- If you are talking with someone, tell the person that you need a few minutes alone.

- Leave the situation.

- Engage in a relaxing activity.

- Return to the person or situation when you feel calmer.

Using Positive Self-Talk

- Identify what statements would be helpful to think about when you feel stress.

- List the statements you currently say to yourself that increase stressful feelings, or don't help you deal with stress. These might include, "I can't do this," or "This is horrible."

- Write out positive statements you can make instead. These might include, "I can handle this," or "This isn't so bad."

- When encountering a stressful situation, repeatedly say the positive statements to yourself.

- If you catch yourself thinking unhelpful thoughts, replace them with positive statements.

Using Body Relaxation Techniques

- Find a quiet spot to lie down or sit back.

- Close your eyes.

- Tense each muscle group for three seconds and then release. This works best if you start from either the top (your head) or the bottom (your toes) and work your way through your body. For example, tense and release all the muscles in your toes and feet first. Then tense and release all the muscles in your ankles and calves, and continue upward.

- Inhale when you tense muscles and hold the breath in; exhale when releasing the tension from muscles.

- Concentrate on how it feels when you relax each muscle.

- During non-stressful times, practice relaxation techniques (at least two times each day).

- When you encounter stressful situations, be aware of which muscle groups are tensed up.

- Exhale and release the tension in those muscles.

Keeping a Journal

- Find a quiet time and place to write.

- Write about the events of the day.

- When writing about stressful situations, explain how you were thinking (your self-talk) and feeling about the situation.

- Include how you could better handle the next stressful situation by using better self-talk statements.

- Write about the relaxation techniques you tried in order to reduce feelings of being overwhelmed.

- Write in a way that allows you to vent your feelings honestly.

- Write in your journal regularly and during stressful times.

Asking for Help *

- Determine if a task or problem is too much for you to handle alone.

- Choose an appropriate person who could best help you.

- Ask the person if he or she would be willing to help you.

MANAGING STRESS

- Describe the problem or task you need help with.
- Allow the person to help in any way he or she can.
- Thank the person for the help.

Rewarding Yourself *

- Decide if you are proud of something you have accomplished.
- If so, tell yourself that you have done a good job and should feel good about it.
- Treat yourself with a self-care activity or give yourself a break.
- Remind yourself of the progress and gains you have made.

CHAPTER 15

Home Safety

PROBLEM: Children are living in an unsafe or unsanitary home environment.

Concerns about unsafe and unsanitary conditions in a home can arise from any number of situations or items. Sometimes, parents or caregivers are not aware of hazards that endanger the children in the home, or are financially unable to make repairs. Educating parents about home safety issues can help them learn how to make their home safer. It also can provide information on how they can obtain assistance in the form of services or funds for necessary repairs and improvements.

Unsanitary living conditions might occur when parents or caregivers haven't been able to give enough attention to cleaning the home, disposing of waste, and taking care of personal hygiene. Sometimes, this can place children at a greater risk of infection, disease, and other harm. In some cases, unclean living conditions make children the target of ridicule and alienation by peers and adults; others may make fun of them, or they might find it difficult to make friends.

Though society's standards for cleanliness and safety may be much higher than conditions that actually pose a danger to children, referring agencies and child welfare professionals usually set minimum safety and sanitation standards for homes where children are living. By following these guidelines and learning the skills offered here, parents can improve their success with basic home safety and cleanliness concerns.

Creating a Safer Home for Children

- Keep poisonous chemicals and medications where children can't reach them.

- Cover all electrical outlets, and repair any exposed or frayed wires. Keep electrical cords out of walkways.

- Keep areas where children can go free of excessive clutter and trash.

- Keep floors, furniture, and toys clean and sanitary.

- Store sharp objects such as knives, glass, tools, and metal where children can't reach them.

- Prevent children from going into unsafe areas of the home and yard.

- Make sure that children can easily get out of the home in case of an emergency.

- Install smoke and carbon monoxide detectors and other safety devices. Keep them in good working order and regularly check their batteries.

- Dispose of animal waste regularly and properly, and always keep it out of the reach of children.

- Store garbage where children can't reach it, and take it out regularly.

- Put dirty dishes in the sink and wash them regularly.

- Make sure children cannot get inside empty or unused large appliances (refrigerators, dryers, freezers, etc.).

- Keep children away from stoves, heaters, ovens, and fireplaces when they are in use or still hot.

- Block stairways with gates, doors, or railings so children cannot fall.

- Make sure children have and wear helmets for activities such as bicycling or skateboarding.

- Write down emergency telephone numbers and keep them near the phone.

- Empty ashtrays regularly.

- Keep matches and lighters out of the reach of children.

- Lock guns, firearms, and other weapons in a safe place. Be sure that guns are unloaded, and store ammunition in a locked and separate location.

Setting a Schedule for Household Chores

- Determine a time frame for the schedule. For example, will the chores be done hourly, daily, weekly, monthly, or at a certain time of day?

- List all the chores that reasonably can be accomplished within the time frames.

- List the chores or tasks in the order that they need to be done.

- Set a time for when chores or tasks should be completed.

- Determine which family members will be responsible for completing each task or chore.

- Write out the chore schedule and put it where everyone can check it.

- If necessary, plan the schedule around activities that already occur regularly, such as watching favorite television shows, meals, or coffee time.

HOME SAFETY

- Occasionally check the schedule.
- Complete chores on the schedule at the times indicated.
- Continue to follow the schedule until everyone remembers to do the chores routinely.

Cleaning House

- Complete housecleaning tasks according to a schedule.
- Look over the home every day to determine what needs to be cleaned immediately, even if that task is not on the schedule.
- Include these tasks in the housecleaning schedule: doing dishes, doing laundry, cleaning or vacuuming floors, changing bedding, picking up, taking out the trash, wiping down counter and table surfaces, dusting, cleaning toilets, washing the tub or shower, and cleaning sinks.
- Adjust the housecleaning schedule as needed.

Doing Laundry

- Gather all dirty clothes, bedding, and towels to be laundered.
- Separate the laundry into three piles: white or very light-colored fabrics, medium-colored fabrics that do not have much dye in them, and dark-colored fabrics.
- Check the washing instructions on the inside tag of each piece of clothing when you're not sure how the fabric should be washed.
- Check and empty all pockets.
- Pre-treat all stains or spots.
- Check the labels on clothing to determine what water temperature they should be washed in. If the label directions are not clear, use these guidelines: Whites go in hot water, medium colors go in warm water, and dark colors go in cold water.

- Fill the clothes washer with water that is the appropriate temperature.

- Put in detergent according to the directions on the container.

- Put clothes in the water. Make sure you don't overload the washer; the clothing should have enough room to agitate freely in the water.

- Shut the lid and start the wash cycle.

- When the washer has completed the full cycle, put the clothes in the dryer or hang them up to dry. Check labels to determine which fabrics can or cannot be heat dried.

- Start another load of laundry in the washer while one load is drying.

- When clean clothes are dry, fold and properly store them in closets or dressers so they don't get mixed with dirty laundry.

Attending to Children's Personal Hygiene

- Set a routine for checking children for cleanliness. For example, check them before school, after supper, or at bedtime.

- Make sure the children have clean bodies and hair. Children should wash their hair and faces regularly, bathe or shower with soap, wash hands, brush teeth, and brush hair.

- Make sure that children are wearing clean clothing, and that the clothes fit and are appropriate for the weather conditions.

- Make sure the children smell clean. If you notice an odor, check to see if it is from dirty clothing or body odor. If it is, have the child change clothes and/or wash.

- If a child is old enough, teach him or her how to wash, and how to pick out appropriate clothing. Help the child if he or she is having difficulties.

- If a child is too young to wash and dress himself or herself, provide help.

Checking for Head Lice

- Recognize the signs of exposure to head lice: child scratches his or her head frequently; child complains that scalp hurts or itches; the child's friends or schoolmates have head lice.

- Under a bright light, look through the child's hair for tiny nits (egg sacks) that are attached tightly to the hair shaft.

- Grasp single strands of hair at the scalp between the fingernails of the thumb and forefinger and gently slide fingernails down the hair shaft. If your fingernail rubs across a small bump that isn't easily removed, it may be a nit.

- Look for very small, almost transparent bugs crawling on or near the scalp.

- If you suspect a child has head lice, take proper precautions so that they don't spread to others. Treat the child and wash his or her bedding immediately.

- Check everyone who lives in the home for head lice, and be prepared to treat all family members.

- Talk to a doctor before treating a child under age three.

- After examining a child for head lice, wash your hands thoroughly with hot water and soap, and scrub under your fingernails.

- Contact the public health department, school nurse, or your family doctor to get further instructions on how to treat a person with head lice.

Planning Fire Escape Routes

- Contact the local fire department for information on making escape plans.

- Make sure that windows and doors to the outside are easy to get to and not blocked.

- Plan other ways to escape in case ground floor exits are blocked or cut off. For example, which windows or doors on the upper floors lead out to a balcony or fire escape ladder?

- Decide where family members will meet outside the home if they are separated during an escape.

- Review with family members all possible escape routes from the home.

- Explain to family members that it is okay to break a window or door in order to make a safe escape. Explain how windows and doors can be safely opened or broken.

- Explain the escape plan to all family members and occasionally review it or make necessary changes.

CHAPTER 16

Community Safety

PROBLEM: Family lives in a high-crime neighborhood.

At-risk families can be vulnerable to many dangers when they are out in the community. Families may live in high-crime neighborhoods where gun violence, gang activity, home break-ins, and drug traffic are common occurrences. They may have trouble trusting public safety officials. Identity theft, cyber bullying, or pornography that may arrive electronically via the Internet or cell phone can also be threats to a family's safety. It is important to help these families realistically assess the dangers they face outside their home and decide how they will address them.

Families need to identify and prioritize their risks. When and where do they feel unsafe? What risks are greatest in their immediate neighborhood? Families then must locate the resources and support services that will help keep them safe or they can turn to in times of need. Does the police department have a community relations officer who knows the area? Is there a local neighborhood watch program? Are there safe and sponsored after-school, weekend, and summer activities available for their children? Finally, parents should create a safety plan that outlines how family members will address areas of concern. The plan could include things such as how to keep children off the streets, what to do if threatened by someone carrying a weapon, or how to decrease the chances of a home break-in.

The following skills suggest steps that practitioners can teach families to take to keep adults and children safe from dangers that threaten them out in the community.

Increasing Family Safety outside the Home

- Identify the unsafe areas outside your home for you and your children.

- Create a plan for when family members must be in unsafe areas (for example, bring a friend, plan to go only during the day, carry pepper spray or a personal alarm).

- Teach your children to be aware of their surroundings and other people, the potential danger of approaching strangers, how to call 911, and which homes and shops in the neighborhood are safe places to go if they feel threatened.

- Teach children the dangers of being around someone with a gun or other dangerous weapon.

- If you or your children are threatened with violence, give the person what he or she is demanding such as a purse, wallet, cell phone, or jewelry.

- Follow the steps to staying calm when you find yourself in situations of conflict or confrontation. Learn to walk away.

- Have family members wear light-colored clothing outside after dark.

- Install motion detector lights outside your home.

- Repair broken windows and door locks immediately.

- If there is a pool or any sort of water (well, river, pond, culvert, etc.) near your home, install door alarms so you know and can monitor your children when they go outside. In-ground pools should be fenced and entrances or ladders to above-ground pools should be blocked.

Monitoring Children's Friends and Activities

- Invite your children's friends into your home in order to meet and get to know them.

- Make an effort to meet the parents of your children's friends by attending school events, neighborhood block parties and gatherings, recreational and sports activities.

- When your children are invited to attend parties, sleepovers, or activities in their friends' homes, contact the parents to confirm the arrangements and that there will be adult supervision.

- Occasionally check on your children to be sure they are where they said they would be.

- Teach your children to ask your permission before leaving home.

- Have your children write where they are going, who they will be with, and when they will return on a chalkboard, dry erase board, or calendar that you post in the home.

Finding Community Safety Resources

- Check with local cell phone companies or stores to see if they have donated phones that can be used for emergencies or look into purchasing a prepaid cell phone.

- Locate after-school and other recreational programs for children offered by organizations like the United Way, Girls and Boys Clubs, the Salvation Army, the public school, and local library and enroll your children in one or more of them.

- Introduce yourself to neighbors. Consider joining or helping to organize a neighborhood watch program.

- On your own or with neighbors, contact the local police's community relations department to discuss neighborhood safety issues and what police can do to help.

- Seek information from local youth safety, community action, gang awareness or prevention groups on other measures you can take to keep your family safe.

- To locate any of the above organizations and agencies, check your telephone directory's front section or yellow pages for listings of Community Service numbers or call 211 (in many communities) to speak with a local referral agency.

Creating a Family Safety Plan

- List one or more of the most immediate and threatening safety issues you feel endanger your children or the family.

- Select and specify which safety goals your family wants to achieve.

- Identify what changes need to be made to reduce the family's risk.

- Determine what actions each family member will take to reach the goals. Discuss these with your children and ask for their ideas.

- Explain to children the reasons why working toward the safety goals is important to them and the family as a whole.

- Establish a timeline for completing each of the actions.

- Write up the plan, have all family members sign it, and post it in an area of the home where all can see and refer to it.

- Review the safety plan regularly (daily, weekly, monthly) and follow up with all family members to check on their progress toward the safety goals.

Protecting against Safety Threats via the Internet and Cell Phones

- If you have a computer, keep it in an open area of the home so you can monitor your children's use of it.

- Visit websites such as **getnetwise.org** for information on keeping your children safe online, filtering unwanted e-mail and spam, protecting personal information, setting your search engine to block pornography, and monitoring your children's website visits.

- Review with children that the following should never be shared online or in text messages to people they do not know personally: name, e-mail or postal address, phone number, photo, school address, etc.

- It is generally not a good idea for you or your child to meet personally with someone you've only met online, but, if you feel it will be safe, arrange to do so only in a public, busy place.

- Identify and post rules for use near the computer.

- Teach children to be responsible for their behavior online and in text messaging (making good choices, reporting concerns to you).

- If your children have pages on Facebook, MySpace, or other social networking sites, discuss with them what is appropriate and what is not appropriate for posting and how to limit access to people they personally know. Know their user names and passwords and periodically monitor the content of their pages.

- If your children have access to a cell phone, discuss the rules and limits of sending text messages, the dangers of cyberbullying, and ask them to tell you immediately if they receive threatening or inappropriate calls or messages from anyone.

- Do not respond to e-mail, chat, or text messages asking for personal information or for you to send money to someone.

Resources

CHAPTER 16

Finding Resources for Families

There are many local, state, federal, public and private organizations, charities, and agencies who offer services for families in need. Many families, however, may be aware of only a small fraction of the resources potentially available to them. As a practitioner, you want to be able to guide parents and children to services that can make a meaningful difference in the quality of their family life.

Finding resources can start with simply checking the local telephone directory or doing a modest amount of research on the Internet. The list that follows includes some ideas and starting points for finding information and appropriate services in your community for the families you work with.

Relationships

Family/Marital Counseling

Families with severe breakdowns in relationships between parents or between parent(s) and children may benefit from family or marital counseling. Find these services in the telephone yellow pages or do an Internet search using terms such as "free family counseling" or "marital therapy" followed by the name of your community and state.

Education

National Head Start Association

Head Start operates more than two thousand private, nonprofit school readiness programs serving a million young children from low-income families across the country. It provides comprehensive education, health, nutrition, and parent involvement services. For more information, visit **nhsa.org**. To locate a program, go to **eclkc.ohs.acf. hhs.gov/hslc/HeadStartOffices** or look up "Head Start" in the telephone book's business white pages.

PTAs/PTOs

Children benefit when their parents are actively involved in their schools and joining the local PTA or PTO can introduce parents to the teachers and staff who work with their kids every day as well as to the parents of their children's friends. Check with the school or visit the school's website for contact information and meeting schedules.

U.S. Department of Education (DOE)

In a special section for parents, the DOE's website, **ed.gov/ parents**, offers advice on preparing a child for school, finding data on schools, locating schools and after-school care, helping a child with special needs, and much more. Parents can also find information on options including school choice and obtaining tutoring help.

United Way of America

Local United Way chapters sponsor programs that support school readiness, literacy, mentoring, after-school, and dropout prevention. To see which services are offered in your community, contact the local chapter (in the telephone book's business white pages or go to **liveunited.org**).

Housing

U.S. Department of Housing and Urban Development (HUD)

HUD's website, **hud.gov**, has extensive information for both home owners and renters. At **hud.gov/renting**, tenants can find help locating affordable rentals, public housing, privately owned subsidized housing, and housing counseling agencies. The website also has links to information on fair housing laws, tenant rights, security deposits, foreclosures, and renters insurance.

Medical and Mental Health Needs

Free Health Care Clinics

Check with the County Health Department to find clinics in your area that provide free or low-cost medical and dental care. (Also see the listings on **freemedicalcamps.com**.) These can either be permanent facilities or several-day events organized by local health care providers. Free flu shots, blood pressure, cholesterol and other screenings are sometimes offered at health fairs, employers' worksites, grocery stores, or other locations.

Substance Abuse and Mental Health Services Administration (SAMHSA)

An agency of the U.S. Department of Health and Human Services, SAMHSA sponsors a website, **samhsa.org**, with information on locating drug and alcohol treatment programs and mental health care providers across the country. Its 24-hour helpline, 1-800-662-HELP (4357) is also available to locate treatment services.

Transportation to Medical Appointments

The U.S. Department of Health and Human Services (see next entry) and Medicaid will sometimes provide bus or subway passes, cab

FINDING RESOURCES

fare, or gas cards that families can use to get to medical and mental health care appointments.

U.S. Department of Health and Human Services (HHS)

The HHS website has several useful sections for parents. At **hhs.gov/children**, parents can find advice on health (for children of all ages, for children with disabilities, locating health care providers and facilities), financial assistance (child support, child care, aid for children with disabilities, temporary assistance for needy families, paying for home heating and cooling, eligibility for federal government benefits), health insurance (Medicaid, State Children's Health Insurance Program), and safety (abuse and neglect, domestic or partner violence, substance abuse, teen violence). At **hhs.gov/safety**, there are links to information on exercise and fitness, diet and nutrition, healthy lifestyle (obesity, smoking, drinking, injury and accident prevention), vaccination/ immunization, health screening, and the environment and health. Parents may also fill out a Family Health History that will identify areas of higher risk for disease, early warning signs, and ways to reduce disease risks.

United Way of America

Local United Way chapters support organizations and agencies that meet basic needs as well as address health insurance coverage, medical and oral health, childhood obesity, substance abuse, family violence, childhood immunizations, and other health and medical issues. For information in your area, find the local chapter in the telephone book's business white pages or go to **liveunited.org**.

Money Management

AnnualCreditReport.com

This is the official site that allows consumers to check their credit report once every twelve months for free from each of the three major nationwide credit reporting companies: Equifax, TransUnion, and Experian.

U.S. Department of Health and Human Services (HHS)

Go to the website, **hhs.gov**, and click on the "Families" button at the top of the page to find a list of financial assistance programs available to needy families and children.

Personal Finance/Budgeting Advice

There are many websites that offer impartial money management advice and downloadable worksheets and calculators. A few include: **money.cnn.com/pf, usa.gov/Citizen/Topics/Money_Taxes.shtml, smartmoney.com/personal-finance, finance.yahoo.com/personal-finance,** and **momsbudget.com**.

Thrift Stores

Clothing, toys, furniture, home furnishings, appliances, and more can be found at bargain prices in thrift stores run by local churches, veterans' organizations, Goodwill, the Salvation Army, and St. Vincent De Paul. Locate them by checking in the telephone directory's yellow pages under "Thrift Stores" or by doing an Internet search for "thrift store" followed by the name of your city or town.

United Way of America

United Way has a Financial Stability Partnership program to help low-income families maximize their income and build savings. Many chapters offer free tax preparation services. Find the local chapter in the telephone book's business white pages or go to **liveunited.org**.

Child Supervision

Boys Town National Hotline

The hotline is a twenty-four-hour/seven-day-a-week service for parents and children who are in crisis or seeking help with a problem. Hotline counselors can refer families who need assistance to services and agencies in their own community. The toll-free number is 1-800-448-3000. The hotline also offers a website (**yourlifeyourvoice.org**) for children and teens where they can ask questions, share their problems, concerns, and challenges, and express themselves through poetry, artwork, photos, and writing.

FINDING RESOURCES

Child Care Aware

This federally funded organization, **childcareaware.org**, can help parents consider child care choices and payment options, find quality child care providers, and join an online network of concerned parents. Child care videos are also available for viewing on the website.

ChildCare.gov

This website is the federal government's official site offering information and advice on child care.

Parenting Information and Classes

Pediatricians may have information about local parenting classes, or you can search the Web for "parenting classes" followed by the name of your community. Books and DVDs with advice for parents can be checked out of public libraries. Websites such as **parenting.org** and **parenthood.com** can answer many parenting questions. Internet-savvy parents may also want to follow and participate in one or more parenting blogs where parents pose and answer questions, share advice, and support each other.

Informal and Formal Support

Administration for Children & Families (ACF)

ACF is a federal agency that funds state, local, and tribal organizations to provide family assistance (welfare), child support, child care, Head Start, child welfare, and other assistance to families. Its website, **acf.hhs.gov**, provides information, listings, and links to state and local agencies which actually provide the services.

Boys and Girls Clubs of America

In addition to sport, recreational and fitness activities, Boys and Girls Clubs offer programs in the arts, environment, health and life skills, careers, character, education, and alcohol, drug, gang and pregnancy prevention. The national organization's website is **bcga.org**.

211 (Community Service Numbers)

If you cannot find the assistance you need, try calling 211 to speak with a local referral agency that can help you locate an appropriate organization or service.

Legal Aid

Many communities have nonprofit organizations of attorneys who offer free legal aid and information on legal rights to low- and moderate-income families with problems related to housing, work, family, bankruptcy, disability, immigration, and other topics. The website **lawhelp.org** has links to information on free legal assistance available in each state.

Parents without Partners

Local chapters of this national organization provide educational, family, and adult social and recreational activities for parents and children from single-parent families. The website, **parentswithoutpartners.org**, can help you find a chapter.

Salvation Army

The Salvation Army provides recreation, rehabilitation, and disaster relief for families through a variety of services – summer youth camps, drug and alcohol counseling, Kroc Community Centers, etc. Their website is **salvationarmyusa.org**.

State and Local Governments

State and Local Government on the Net, **statelocalgov.net**, is an Internet directory of all U.S. state, county, and city government websites.

Nutrition

Farmers Markets

Fresh, locally grown or produced fruits, vegetables, herbs, baked goods, cheese, eggs, meat, and other food can be obtained in season at good prices from farmers markets in many cities. Check the local newspaper for market listings in your area or go to the U.S. Department of Agriculture's website at **ams.usda.gov/ farmersmarkets**.

Food Pantries

Look for the location of food pantries in the telephone book's yellow pages under "Food Banks" or "Food Pantries." Feeding America (formerly known as Second Harvest) has a list of local pantries on its website at **FeedingAmerica.org**.

Food Stamps

Now known as SNAP (Supplemental Nutrition Assistance Program), this federal program provides electronic benefit transfer cards (EBTs) to low-income families for purchasing food. Applications are made through the states, but information on applying and state hotline numbers are available at this website: **fns.usda.gov/FSP**.

Grocery Stores

Many grocery store chains have dietitians or nutritionists on staff who answer customer questions, offer cooking classes, or create in-store and e-mail newsletters offering food and nutrition advice.

MyPyramid.gov

This website, from the U.S. Department of Agriculture, discusses current dietary guidelines, explains and answers questions about the major food groups, outlines nutrition needs of children according to their age, and has links to other useful resources. It includes interactive tools to create individual dietary plans, track what families eat, and plan healthy menus.

Nutrition.gov

This website offers information on shopping, cooking, meal planning, weight management, dietary supplements, and more.

Abuse

Child Welfare Information Gateway

At the website, **childwelfare.gov**, this service of the Children's Bureau, Administration for Children and Families, U.S. Department of Health and Human Services, offers information on preventing, responding to and reporting child abuse and neglect. It includes a state-by-state listing of child abuse reporting numbers.

Hotlines

There are several national hotlines dedicated to victims of various forms of abuse. Their websites offer helpful information on the signs of abuse, how to report it, and advice for abuse survivors. Local hotlines are listed in the telephone directory.

Domestic Violence:

National Domestic Violence Hotline,
1-800-799-SAFE (7233), **ndvh.org**

Child Abuse:

Childhelp National Child Abuse Hotline,
1-800-4-A-CHILD (1-800-422-4453), **childhelp.org**
Safe Horizon, 1-800-621-HOPE (4673), **safehorizon.org**
Boys Town National Hotline, 1-800-448-3000,
boystown.org

Sexual Abuse:

Rape, Abuse, & Incest National Network,
1-800-656-HOPE (4673), **rainn.org**

National Coalition against Domestic Violence

The coalition's website, **ncadv.org**, has information about domestic violence, advice for battered women on how to find help, and a list of state organizations.

National/State Sex Offender Registry

You can access this registry by going to the website operated by the Department of Justice (**fbi.gov/hq/cid/cac/registry.htm**) or

Family Watchdog (**familywatchdog.us**) and enter your city, state, street address, and ZIP code to search for offenders living in your neighborhood.

Parents Anonymous

This support group helps parents who have abused or are afraid they will abuse their children. To locate a local group, go to the website, **parentsanonymous.org**.

Stress

Hotlines

Telephone directories usually have a "Community Service Numbers" page in their front section where local and national hotlines and helplines are listed. Parents and children in crisis or with a problem can also call the Boys Town National Hotline at 1-800-448-3000 for help and referrals.

Medline Plus

At **nlm.nih.gov/medlineplus/stress.html**, this website has many links to information about the prevention and treatment of family and individual stress.

Home Safety

Food, Product Recalls

The website **recalls.gov** gathers all information on government recalls and safety warnings on toys, children's clothing, food, medicine, appliances, motor vehicles, and more.

Home Safety Council

This nonprofit organization's website, **homesafetycouncil. org**, offers checklists, tips, videos, and a home safety guide for parents. Special sections focus on safety for babies and toddlers and preschool through middle school children.

Safe Kids Worldwide

This network of organizations is dedicated to helping protect children from accidental injuries. Their website, **safekids.org**, offers tips on preventing injuries from airway obstructions, bike, car, and pedestrian accidents, falls, fires, poison, and drowning.

Community Safety

American Red Cross

If families are victims of a natural disaster (fire, flood, hurricane, tornado, etc.), they can find assistance from the local chapter of the American Red Cross. Find its location by looking in the telephone book's business white pages. The Red Cross offers training in CPR, first aid, caregiving, babysitting, HIV AIDS education, swimming and water safety, as well as disaster education and preparedness. Learn more at **redcross.org.**

National Crime Prevention Council

Information for parents on this nonprofit's website at **ncpc.org** includes these topics and more: neighborhood and school safety, gangs, bullying, leaving kids home alone, child abductions, Internet safety, identity theft, what to teach kids about strangers, drug abuse, gun safety, conflict management, etc. Their website for kids, **McGruff.org**, features games, videos, advice, downloadable posters, and a safety club children can join.

FINDING RESOURCES

Skills-at-a-Glance Table

Skills, Page Number	Communication	Relationships	Education	Housing	Medical/Mental Health Needs	Money Management	Child Supervision	Informal/Formal Support	Nutrition	Preventing Abuse	Managing Stress	Home Safety	Community Safety
Accessing public assistance and other available resources, 71	■	■	■	■	■	■	■	■	■	■	■	■	■
Active listening, 20	■	■	■	■	■	■	■	■	■	■	■	■	■
Administering medication, 60	■				■		■						
Advocating for a child's education, 43	■		■				■						
Apologizing, 21	■	■						■			■		
Applying for a job, 67	■					■							
Asking about a child's activities, 78	■	■	■				■				■		
Asking children about personal safety, 104	■						■				■		■
Asking for help, 115	■	■	■	■	■	■	■	■	■	■	■	■	■
Asking others for opinions, 21	■	■	■	■	■	■	■		■	■	■		
Attending to children's personal hygiene, 123	■		■		■		■					■	
Baby proofing your home, 78							■					■	
Being a wise consumer, 73			■			■					■		
Being assertive, 22	■	■	■	■	■	■	■	■	■	■	■	■	■
Being prepared for a landlord foreclosure, 52				■		■							
Checking for head lice, 124			■		■		■						
Checking on a child's school progress, 38	■		■				■	■					
Choosing a medical or mental health professional or facility, 58	■				■		■		■				
Choosing an education program, 42	■		■										
Choosing appropriate foods for babies and toddlers, 94					■				■				
Choosing relaxation techniques, 113											■		
Cleaning house, 122				■								■	
Communicating with school personnel, 40	■		■				■	■	■				

149

Skills, Page Number	Communication	Relationships	Education	Housing	Medical/Mental Health Needs	Money Management	Child Supervision	Informal/Formal Support	Nutrition	Preventing Abuse	Managing Stress	Home Safety	Community Safety
Communicating with your child's caregiver, 80	■				■		■	■					
Complimenting, 28	■	■					■	■					
Cooperating with the school when a child breaks a rule, 41	■		■				■	■					
Correcting another person, 24	■	■					■	■					
Creating a balanced menu, 94						■			■				
Creating a family safety plan, 130	■				■		■					■	■
Creating a safer home for children, 120				■	■		■		■			■	
Deciding who to ask for help, 87	■	■	■	■	■	■	■	■	■	■	■	■	■
Developing a social support network, 88	■	■					■	■			■		
Doing laundry, 122												■	
Ending an argument, 24	■	■									■		
Engaging in self-care activities, 112										■	■		
Enrolling in a General Equivalency Diploma (GED) or career training program, 45	■		■										
Establishing a safety plan, 106	■						■			■		■	■
Establishing relationship boundaries, 87	■	■					■	■		■	■		
Expressing feelings, 21	■	■						■			■		
Finding a support group, 90	■	■					■	■		■	■		
Finding child care, 79	■						■	■			■		
Finding community safety resources, 129	■												■
Finding housing, 48	■			■		■						■	■
Fulfilling a lease or rental agreement, 50	■			■		■						■	■
Getting a child immunized, 62	■		■		■								

Skills, Page Number	Communication	Relationships	Education	Housing	Medical/Mental Health Needs	Money Management	Child Supervision	Informal/Formal Support	Nutrition	Preventing Abuse	Managing Stress	Home Safety	Community Safety
Getting involved in community activities, 89	■	■	■				■	■			■		■
Getting involved with a child's school, 40	■		■				■	■					
Getting physically active, 113	■	■			■		■	■			■		
Getting utility services started, 49	■			■								■	
Giving an instruction, 23	■	■					■			■			
Handling landlord disputes, 51	■			■		■						■	■
Helping children make new friends, 35	■	■	■				■	■					
Helping siblings get along with each other, 34	■	■					■	■			■		
Hiring a babysitter, 80	■						■	■			■	■	
Hiring a tutor, 44	■		■				■						
Holding family meetings, 27	■	■					■				■		
Identifying own feelings, 20	■	■						■		■	■		
Improving relationships with your children, 33	■	■					■			■	■		
Increasing family safety outside the home, 128	■						■	■					■
Keeping a journal, 115	■				■					■	■		
Keeping children healthy, 60					■		■						
Keeping medical or mental health appointments, 59	■				■		■				■		
Keeping track of medications, 61	■				■		■					■	
Locating registered sex offenders, 104							■			■			■
Making a late payment, 70	■			■		■							
Making a request, 22	■	■	■	■	■	■	■	■	■	■	■	■	■
Making friends, 86	■	■	■	■			■	■		■	■		

Skills, Page Number	Communication	Relationships	Education	Housing	Medical/Mental Health Needs	Money Management	Child Supervision	Informal/Formal Support	Nutrition	Preventing Abuse	Managing Stress	Home Safety	Community Safety
Managing time, 112			■	■		■			■		■	■	
Monitoring a child's activities (younger children), 77	■	■	■				■	■		■		■	■
Monitoring a child's homework, 38	■		■				■						
Monitoring a child's school attendance, 39	■		■				■						
Monitoring a child's whereabouts (older children), 76	■	■	■				■	■		■		■	■
Monitoring an infant, 78		■					■					■	
Monitoring children in the presence of a potential perpetrator, 103		■						■			■		
Monitoring children's friends and activities, 129	■	■	■				■	■					
Monthly budgeting, 67				■		■			■				
Negotiating, 25	■	■	■				■	■	■				
Notifying others of a change of address, 50	■		■					■					
Obtaining medical or mental health advice, 57	■				■			■					
Offering help, 88	■	■	■					■		■			
Opening a checking account, 68	■					■							
Paying a bill, 69				■		■							
Paying off a debt, 70	■			■		■							
Planning ahead for meals, 94					■	■			■				
Planning fire escape routes, 125	■		■									■	
Praising, 27	■	■	■	■	■	■	■	■	■	■	■	■	■
Pre-approving a child's friends or places to go, 76	■	■	■				■	■		■			
Preparing a meal, 96					■				■			■	
Preparing for a discussion, 25	■	■	■	■	■	■	■	■	■	■	■	■	■
Prioritizing, 66			■	■	■	■			■	■		■	■

Skills, Page Number	Communication	Relationships	Education	Housing	Medical/Mental Health Needs	Money Management	Child Supervision	Informal/Formal Support	Nutrition	Preventing Abuse	Managing Stress	Home Safety	Community Safety
Protecting against safety threats via the internet and cell phone, 131	■	■						■					■
Recognizing medical needs, 56	■				■	■				■	■	■	
Recognizing mental health needs, 57	■				■	■				■	■		
Recognizing stressors, 112	■	■				■				■	■		
Registering a child for school, 43	■		■	■				■					
Reporting abuse, 106	■				■		■	■		■			
Responding to a child's disclosure about abuse, 105	■	■			■			■		■			
Responding to a landlord foreclosure, 52	■			■		■							
Responding to accusations, 24	■	■	■	■	■	■	■	■	■	■	■	■	■
Responding to domestic violence, 107	■	■			■					■	■		
Rewarding yourself, 116	■	■	■	■	■	■	■	■	■	■	■	■	■
Saving money, 69	■			■		■							
Saying "No", 23	■	■					■	■		■	■		
Seeking marriage or family counseling, 32	■	■			■	■	■	■		■	■		
Seeking support when dealing with abuse, 106	■				■		■	■		■	■		
Setting a schedule for household chores, 121	■			■						■	■		
Setting boundaries, 102	■	■					■	■		■			
Setting up a budget, 66				■		■			■				
Setting up exchange systems (cooperative borrowing), 89	■				■	■	■	■			■	■	
Shopping for bargains, 70						■			■				
Shopping for groceries, 95						■			■				
Showing appreciation, 27	■	■	■	■	■	■	■	■	■	■	■	■	■
Signing a lease, 49	■			■								■	■

Skills, Page Number	Communication	Relationships	Education	Housing	Medical/Mental Health Needs	Money Management	Child Supervision	Informal/Formal Support	Nutrition	Preventing Abuse	Managing Stress	Home Safety	Community Safety
Stating expectations, 23	■	■	■	■	■	■	■	■	■	■	■	■	■
Storing food, 96					■				■			■	
Strengthening the relationship with your spouse, 32	■	■					■	■			■		
Taking a time-out, 114	■										■		
Teaching children about appropriate touch, 102	■						■			■			
Transporting children in a car, 81	■		■	■	■		■						
Understanding and avoiding emotional abuse of children, 101	■	■			■		■			■	■		
Understanding and avoiding physical abuse of children, 100	■	■			■		■			■	■		
Understanding and using credit appropriately, 72						■							
Understanding domestic violence, 107	■	■								■	■	■	
Understanding health insurance or Medicaid coverage, 59	■				■	■							
Using a daily assignment book, 39	■		■				■	■					
Using a food pantry, 72				■			■	■	■				
Using body relaxation techniques, 114											■		
Using positive self-talk, 114	■										■		
Using temporary housing (homeless shelters), 51				■				■					
Visiting a child's school, 41	■		■				■	■	■				
Washing dishes, 97					■					■		■	
Writing a contract, 26	■	■	■	■			■	■					

154

Bibliography

Dowd, T., & Tierney, J. (2005). **Teaching Social Skills to Youth: A step-by-step guide to 182 basic to complex skills plus helpful teaching techniques.** Boys Town, NE: Boys Town Press.

    Includes a curriculum of 182 social skills, from basic to complex, broken down into component behaviors for easy use. Explains techniques for teaching individually or in groups and how to plan skill-based treatment interventions for youth with difficult problems such as substance abuse, aggression, running away, depression, or attention deficits.

Burke, R., Herron, R., & Barnes, B.A. (2006). **Common Sense Parenting®.** Boys Town, NE: Boys Town Press.

    Shows parents how to build close relationships with their children, how to prevent or reduce problem behavior by teaching them appropriate ways of behaving, how to stay calm and teach children self-control, and how to develop consistent expectations and consequences for children. (Audio book also available.)

Barnes, B.A. & York, S.M. (2001). **Common Sense Parenting of Toddlers and Preschoolers.** Boys Town, NE: Boys Town Press.

    Tells parents how to balance nurturing behaviors that demonstrate love and affection with the discipline all young children need to learn and thrive. (Audio book also available.)

Resetar Volz, J., Snyder, T., & Sterba, M. (2009). **Teaching Social Skills to Youth with Mental Health Disorders: Incorporating social skills into treatment planning for 109 disorders.** Boys Town, NE: Boys Town Press.

Includes 109 disorders commonly diagnosed in youth, with lists of social skills that can be targeted during treatment of each disorder. Treatment plans that incorporate social skill instruction from a group home, mental health facility, and a school are offered.

Munger, R.L. (2005). **Changing Children's Behavior by Changing the People, Places, and Activities in Their Lives.** Boys Town, NE: Boys Town Press.

Identifies ten "behavior settings" in which children and adolescents spend most of their time – home, neighborhood, school, after-school, electronic, friends, work, faith, recreation and leisure, and sports – and discusses how changes in these environments and the people in them can impact youths' behavior.

Peterson, J. L., Kohrt, P. E., Shadoin, L. M., & Authier, K. J. (1995). **Building Skills in High-Risk Families: Strategies for the home-based practitioner.** Boys Town, NE: Boys Town Press.

Provides strategies for working in the home with high-risk families. Shows how to establish relationships, identify and build on family strengths, use intervention techniques such as role playing, confrontation, metaphors, contracting and reframing, teach skills to solve difficult problems, and create individualized treatment plans.

Index